The Boston Globe

This book is available in quantity at special discounts for your group or organization. For further information, contact:

Triumph Books
542 South Dearborn Street, Suite 750
Chicago, Illinois 60605
Phone: (312) 939-3330
Fax: (312) 663-3557

Printed in the United States of America
ISBN: 978-1-57243-979-5

Credits

WRITERS Joe Concannon, Paul Harber, Jackie MacMullan, Jim McCabe, Michael Vega.

PHOTOGRAPHERS Paul R. Benoit, 81 • Pam Berry, 130 • John Blanding, 7, 30, 100 • Sarah Brezinsky, 98 • Barry Chin, 5, 71, 103, 138, 151, 157 • Jim Davis, 70, 87, 138, 141, 158 • J.D. Denham, 34 • Danny Goshtigian, 124 • Bill Greene, 42, 45, 70 • Pat Greenhouse, 97 • Tom Herde, front cover, 26, 35, 48, 95, 105 • Erik Jacobs, 133 • David Kamerman, 39, 123, 147, 156, 157 • Robert E. Klein, 139 • Suzanne Kreiter, 17 • Tom Landers, 41, 46, 47, 53, 54, 56, 58, 115, 138 • Matthew J. Lee, 27, 57, 76-78, 113, 138, 143, 147 • Wendy Maeda, 23, 41, 155, 157 • Patricia McDonnell, 119 • Frank O'Brien, 14-16, 20, 22, 43, 44, 51, 55, 83, 107, 116, 134, 136, 138, 150, 153, 156, 157 • Peter Pereira, 92 • Bill Polo, 29 • Joanne Rathe, 2, 56, 88 • Evan Richman, 18 • George Rizer, 126 • Stephen Rose, 10, 50 • Dina Rudick, 28 • David L. Ryan, 19, 98, 99, 149 • Laurie Swope, 84 • Shawn Thew, 52 • John Tlumacki, 9, 40, 69, 70 • Jonathan Wiggs, 5, 145.

ADDITIONAL PHOTOS COURTESY OF AP/Wide World Photos, 37, 64, 67, 72, 98, 120, 146, 154, back cover • Boston Globe files, 35, 51, 62, 65, 96, 108, 109, 125 • Boston Golf Club, 31 • Francis Ouimet Scholarship Fund, 36, 134 • Samoset Resort, 25 • Worcester Country Club, 66 • Yale University, 32.

WITH SPECIAL THANKS TO The Boston Globe sports department, photo and design departments, and library staff.

Book Staff

EDITOR Janice Page
ART DIRECTOR/DESIGNER Rena Anderson Sokolow
RESEARCHER Ben Cafardo
COPY EDITOR Ron Driscoll
IMAGING Frank Bright

FRONT COVER Playing Highland Golf Links in Truro, Massachusetts, with Highland (Cape Cod) Light as a backdrop.
OPPOSITE PAGE Leonard Thompson and anxious onlookers assess his efforts to work around a tree during the 2005 Bank of America Championship.
BACK COVER Brad Faxon celebrates his dramatic playoff victory at the 2005 Buick Championship in Cromwell, Connecticut.

Golfing New England

Contents

MAKING A SPLASH at the Sandbar Open Golf
Tournament in Ipswich, Massachusetts.

Fall is the best time of the year in New England. The weather is perfect, leaves start to change colors and the greens are at their smoothest. Golfers capitalize when Indian summer arrives, knowing that the season is almost over.

My best memories of golf as a kid revolve around late fall days, playing a quick 18 (with the leaf rule, of course) and moving swiftly to beat darkness. Every day was a bonus, and I've always felt that those days helped me fall in love with golf and established me as a budding player when I was still a junior.

The most commonly asked question I get as a PGA Tour player is: "How did you make it growing up in Rhode Island?"

I laugh and quickly tell the inquiring mind that it didn't hurt Arnold Palmer (Pennsylvania), Jack Nicklaus (Ohio) or Tom Watson (Kansas). I experienced a golf landscape much like those legends had grown up on years earlier.

In New England, the season could be seven months or 12, depending on Mother Nature, but playing in harsh conditions makes one stronger. I cherish those boyhood memories of playing New England golf in less-than-ideal conditions. The wind would blow, temperatures would fall, and making a full swing with layers of sweaters was a serious challenge. But onward we would play and it was that crusty old New England attitude that I loved. People thrived on going out when conditions were dismal — and they did so as much for the social importance as for the passionate competition.

Several years after I started playing competitive golf as a junior, I began to fall in love with other aspects of the game — the history, golf course architecture, and most of all, the players, both nationally and locally. My heroes were men such as Bobby Jones and Francis Ouimet, as well as Jack and Arnold, but I loved reading about the contemporary local players and I followed their scores in the New England tournaments.

Hanging around Rhode Island Country Club as a young caddie and locker room assistant — back in the days when Dana Quigley was larger than life to those of us in the Ocean State — I learned more than a 14-year-old probably deserved to. Members would talk about golf all the time and I felt that any story connected to this great game was worth a listen. There's a romantic flavor to golf, a game filled with an endless list of wonderful characters, and perhaps more than other sports it lends itself to charming and intriguing stories.

And, yes, it is a sport that can ignite a great debate or two, so to answer those folks who wonder which are my favorite New England courses, here's my Top 10:

Eastward Ho!, Boston Golf Club, Newport Country Club, The Country Club, The Kittansett Club, Salem Country Club, Rhode Island Country Club, Wannamoisett Country Club, Bay Club at Mattapoisett, and Old Sandwich Golf Club.

Even as I submit those names, I'm torn, for there are so many other great courses in New England. Charming places such as Cape Arundel in Kennebunkport, Maine, or TPC River Highlands in Cromwell, Connecticut (where I won a PGA Tour event in 2005), and how can we forget Nantucket's magnificent Sankaty Head and Nantucket Golf Club?

But just as a list of great courses in New England shouldn't be limited to 10, a compilation of great golf stories should be given ample space. That is what this book has accomplished.

As a native New Englander, I've always felt that when you wanted to read about Boston sports, you had to turn to The Boston Globe. Now, from their pages, they have brought back to life some of the great New England golf stories and the people who have contributed so much to the game.

Years after winning junior tournaments in Massachusetts and Rhode Island, and roughly a quarter century into my PGA Tour career, I still find myself captivated by great golf stories — particularly those that have our beloved New England as a backdrop.   —BRAD FAXON

JIM MCCABE (left) caddies for Pat Burke in 1997.

Introduction

My father was my best friend, and the glue to our relationship was Red Sox baseball. He would regale me with stories of Ted Williams and the heartache of a 1948 playoff loss that haunted him years later. ("Denny Galehouse? How could he pitch Denny Galehouse?" my father would periodically moan about Joe McCarthy's infamous managerial decision.) Season tickets in the 1960s and early 1970s were a prized possession.

Still, if there was a single most cherished gift in my life, it was the golf clubs given to me for my 16th birthday. They led me from the ball fields behind Squantum School in Quincy, Massachusetts, to the fairways of Furnace Brook Golf Club and Ponkapoag Golf Course, and introduced me to a world that has enchanted me ever since.

There is a romanticism to golf that captivates me, for while it is impossible to master the game, it is the never-ending quest to do so that I cannot shake. Being a sportswriter is the only occupational dream I ever had, and writing about golf is a privilege I don't take lightly.

The late Robin Romano, an assistant sports editor at The Boston Globe, is the one to whom I am most indebted. During a round of golf at Presidents Golf Course in Quincy, she not only showed me how brilliant a player she was but encouraged me to follow my passion.

"The game," she said, "will introduce you to so many people with so many great stories."

From the marshals I've come to know at Augusta National to the caddies who stepoff yardages on their days off, from the majesty of Pebble Beach to the historic sod of St. Andrews, my golf travels since the mid-1990s have proved Romano correct, though all of it starts here in New England, where we are most committed to our golf.

Historians have provided us with dates to corroborate the full depth of our area's golf connections. There is evidence that Governor William Burnett arrived in Massachusetts from England in the 1720s with possessions that included a set of golf clubs. More extensive are the documents from the 1880s and 1890s that detail the design of local golf clubs and the playing of the game in Rhode Island, Vermont, and Massachusetts.

But how exactly does one quantify our love for the sport? By visiting the people who have made this game an integral part of their lives and exploring the places where they have played their golf as much for the camaraderie as for the competition.

The passion for golf in New England can be felt on a winter's day on Cape Cod, where you are sure to find foursomes thrilled that it's gotten up to 40 degrees and down to blowing just 15 miles per hour. It can be felt at the New England Senior Golfers' Association's Jarboe Bowl Championship, where 70-year-old competitors must pay respect to those who are in their 80s and 90s and still swinging away. It can be felt in the annual clinic at MGA Links at Mamantapett, where volunteers give golf guidance to children from the Perkins School for the Blind. And it can be felt in the annual proceeding at Winchester Country Club, where the oldest father-and-son tournament in the country is not only an annual staple, it is as integral to summer as the Fourth of July.

New England has played host to champion golfers including Harry Vardon, Bobby Jones, Arnold Palmer, and Tiger Woods. Francis Ouimet and Julius Boros are native New Englanders, and the grandest course designer of them all, Donald Ross, left his indelible mark on our landscape with a long list of brilliant layouts.

When we play it as it lies in New England, we do so off of pine needles and dusty dirt, mud and sand, plush green grass and hardpan. We know tree-lined fairways and wind-swept terrain, cold wet springs and pulsating hot summers. Mostly, we know Mother Nature will interrupt our golfing passion for months at a time with unplayable winters.

That is OK. Absence makes the heart grow fonder.
—JIM McCABE

places
in the
heart

four editions of the PGA Tour's newest marquee stop, the Deutsche Bank Championship, had been played at TPC Boston in Norton, Massachusetts, when plans were announced in 2006 for a sweeping redesign of the young layout. New bunkers, softer doglegs, and different green complexes were at the heart of the changes. The expected end result: TPC Boston would look more like a New England golf course.

If the move had people scratching their heads, it shouldn't have. After all, there is something unique about living in New England — from the beaches to the mountains to the weather we must endure — and so many of these nuances extend to the multitude of golf courses that have graced our landscape for more than 100 years.

In Massachusetts alone there are more than 300 golf courses. And, remarkably, about a quarter of them have celebrated centennials. While they come in all shapes and sizes, there is one thing most have in common: They look like New England golf courses.

And just what does a New England golf course look like? Like it's been there forever.

It could be a piece of land that features rolling fairways framed on both sides by tall trees, or it could be wind-swept terrain that evokes Scotland. The bunkers are well-placed but rustic, the greens are on the small side, and hideous carries over water are at a minimum. It is, above all, natural and beautiful, unpretentious and straight-forward — qualities in keeping with traditional New England.

Choosing 18 spots that are definitively New England is an impossible task (there are hundreds), just as choosing 18 great golf holes is strictly a matter of taste. Still, in the following pages we offer our course picks, along with a full complement of holes chosen by some prominent local golfers for a series first published by The Boston Globe in 2001. These randomly ordered lists are not about finding a "top course" or a "best hole"; they're just about highlighting some of the many things we love about golf in New England. The huge number of worthy runners-up speaks volumes about the care so many people have put into this game, and the courses on which we play it.   —J.M.

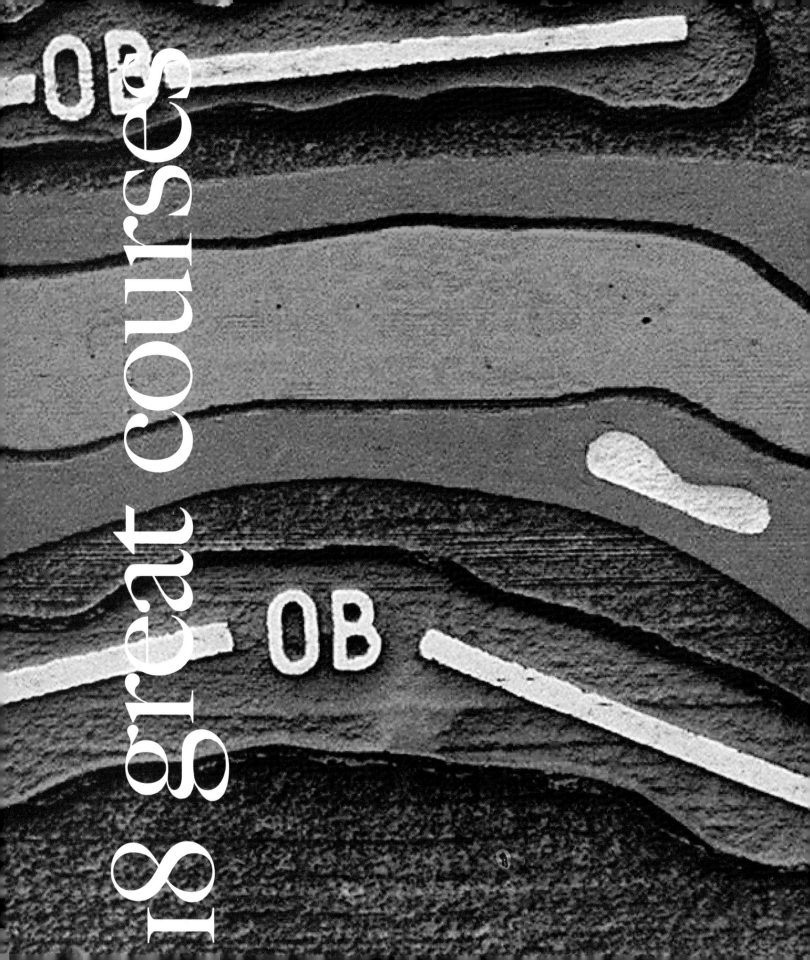

18 great courses

FRANKLIN PARK

FRANKLIN PARK,
MASSACHUSETTS

· None other than the incomparable Bobby Jones thought the uphill, dogleg left 12th hole at this urban oasis was a work of art. It's easy to feel a kinship to Jones, who used to play this parkland course during his graduate school days at Harvard. Truth be told, though, you'll probably fall for the firm and fast conditions over the course of the first 11 holes. And the feeling never wanes. If anything, most golfers gain more respect for this place with every round.

THE COUNTRY CLUB,
MASSACHUSETTS

You may not hear voices when you turn off of Clyde Street, but if you have a keen appreciation for the game, surely you'll feel a sort of spiritual presence here. This is where the game came to life in the United States; when former caddie Francis Ouimet walked across the street from his house and won the US Open in 1913 at The Country Club, the game was introduced to the masses. A founding member of the US Golf Association, The Country Club is 27 holes of unpretentiousness — golf for the sake of golf.

MIKE SHEERIN

MYOPIA HUNT CLUB, MASSACHUSETTS

You don't "play golf" at this masterpiece so much as you embrace a golf experience. From the 275-yard, uphill par-4 first to the par-4 18th that features a sort of island green surrounded by devilish bunkers, your round of golf at Myopia is unlike anywhere else. Brilliant bunkers, many of them haphazardly placed, and green contours that are unique and brutally challenging are at the heart of H.C. Leeds's design, which dates back to 1896. Vibrant fescue is at every turn of the head. Don't bother looking for a course with more character; it doesn't exist.

HIGHLAND LINKS,
MASSACHUSETTS

To go back in time, golf-wise, you have to drive to the very eastern tip of Massachusetts, way down on the Lower Cape, just shy of Provincetown. It is nine holes of pure joy, a hidden gem (pictured additionally on this book's cover) tucked into sand dunes on a bluff some 130 feet above the ocean. Oh, it measures a mere 2,650 yards, that is true, but leave the ego in the car and rely, instead, on imagination. You'll be rewarded with a newfound respect for the game.

KEN LEWIS

DENNIS PINES GOLF COURSE, MASSACHUSETTS

Public golf at its finest, this facility should be the model for the industry to show off. If you love golf, you are always welcomed at "The Pines," where it matters not whether you are young or old, male or female; it matters only that you want to put the peg in the ground. Doglegs are the main fare, which forces you to think twice on all tee shots, and after one or two misfires, you'll no doubt discover enough pine straw to understand how they came up with the name for the course 40 years ago.

SAMOSET RESORT, MAINE

Sprawling views of Penobscot Bay are at the heart of this magnificent property that has been a destination point for those seeking rest and relaxation for more than 100 years. Maine native Bradley Booth oversaw some much-needed restoration and redesign work a few years ago, and the changes only enhanced what is a lavish experience. Wind through a few tree-lined holes, play out along the daunting Penobscot, and all the while soak in the unmatched air of northern New England. Top it off with a visit to nearby Camden and you've completed what ranks as a perfect day.

marion

MEREDITH KOTOWSKI

THE KITTANSETT CLUB,
MASSACHUSETTS

Anyone privileged with a chance to play this jewel along Buzzards Bay will likely wake up thinking about the tee shot at No. 3 — as glorious a par 3 as there is. It's 165 yards, either over ocean water or sandy beach, depending upon the tide. But this majestic seaside layout has so much more to offer than just that one shot. There are sweeping seaside views and lush native grasses, and an understated clubhouse that oozes so much character you'll want to sit on the veranda for hours.

south hadley

THE ORCHARDS,
MASSACHUSETTS

Any serious list of Donald Ross designs will have this Western Massachusetts layout prominently displayed, and it may well be his most underrated work. Sitting on property owned by Mount Holyoke College, The Orchards was for years semi-private but is now fully private. It features a Ross staple — deep bunkers with grass faces — and tight driving holes make for a compelling challenge. If it were in the Boston area, it would demand greater attention. But on its own great merit, it was deemed worthy enough to host the 2004 US Women's Open.

MICHELLE WIE

NEWPORT COUNTRY CLUB,
RHODE ISLAND

The drive up to the club-house is so awe-inspiring that at any second you expect to spot Jay Gatsby and Daisy Buchanan meandering out on the front lawn. Great as it is, however, the clubhouse architecture becomes a distant memory when you explore the golf course, which owes its creation to members of the Vanderbilt and Astor families. Saturated in history (the US Open and US Amateur were introduced here in 1895), Newport CC is arguably the finest in New England, a marvelously firm and fast seaside links course when it is at its very best.

STOW ACRES,
MASSACHUSETTS

It was before the building of golf courses became widespread, maybe 20 years ago, and if you were serious about your golf and wanted a challenge, you came to this small country town northwest of Boston. The North Course was longer, the South Course a true risk/reward layout; but no matter which one you played, the trip was worth it. All these years later, no matter that a host of terrific daily-fee facilities have opened, Stow Acres remains a must-play for true golfers. Vintage tree-lined fairways, small greens, elevation changes, and exquisite conditions make for an unforgettable experience.

If it's good enough for a former president and a quartet of major champions, it should be good enough for you, right? Truth is, this storied golf course was a great one long before George H.W. Bush teed it up here; it's just that he's been passionate about spreading the word. And when a president extends an invitation, people accept. Thus have champions Phil Mickelson, Fred Couples, Davis Love III, and Justin Leonard basked in the charm of this 5,881-yard, par-69 Walter Travis design that commands shot-making precision.

kennebunk

hingham

BOSTON GOLF CLUB, MASSACHUSETTS

They didn't build this golf course a hundred years ago; it only looks as if they did. Gil Hanse studied the great golf courses of Scotland, and his stylish design work with rugged terrain in the woods off Route 53 proves that he learned his lessons well. Carts are not allowed, caddies are mandatory, and the attention to detail is never ending. Opened in 2004, this private venue is a testament to patience and diligence, and it pays homage to the features that make golf so great.

port

THE COURSE AT YALE, CONNECTICUT

Harvard can always try to win The Game, but it can never match its archrival when it comes to golf, for Yale has The Course. And what a gem it is. Designed in 1924 by the heralded Charles Blair Macdonald and Seth Raynor, The Course at Yale is one distinct hole after another, with particularly strong par 3s. The 146-yard fifth is surrounded by three deep bunkers and the 235-yard ninth features a green 65 yards deep. Built over hundreds of acres of woods and rolling terrain, the golf course has stood the test of time and confounded the world's best players.

13

new haven

PORTSMOUTH COUNTRY CLUB, NEW HAMPSHIRE

It is a difficult task to stand close to a bustling highway like I-95 and feel secluded, but that is the magical appeal of this course designed by Robert Trent Jones, Sr. Everything about Portsmouth CC is pure golf, from the holes that wind around Great Bay, to the demanding drives out of chutes, to the cozy par 3s on your inward nine. The club dates back to 1901, but it was forced to relocate to its present locale in 1956, and it would be hard to argue that Jones was not on top of his game in this task.

JARED LAMOTHE

SAKONNET GOLF CLUB,
RHODE ISLAND

You want a testament to Donald Ross's brilliance? Forget Pinehurst No. 2; consider, instead, that the famed architect (right) chose for many years to spend his summers right here on the water, just over the Massachusetts border. Get a chance to come here and you'll offer even more respect to Ross. Sakonnet is the definition of quaint, a course under 6,000 yards that offers as much challenge as you can handle, thanks to narrow fairways, fantastic bunkers, and small, fast greens. Ross designed it in 1899 and drew inspiration for many of his other projects as he walked the grounds.

WOODSTOCK COUNTRY CLUB,
VERMONT

In 1961, Robert Trent Jones Sr. took a golf course that dated back to 1895 and redesigned it. He did a commendable job, for its 6,000 yards offer plenty of challenges, including five holes in which water is in play. But thankfully, he did not modernize the town, as it remains the consummate New England locale. With the Green Mountains offering a scenic backdrop, the golf is terrific, but indulge yourself: Strolls across the Village Green, a stop into Laurance Rockefeller's Woodstock Inn (left), and irresistible lobster crab cake sandwiches are a perfect complement.

EKWANOK COUNTRY CLUB,
VERMONT

Tucked away in a state more closely identified with skiing than golf, Ekwanok is true New England — anonymous to the masses, but its history and flavor are well known in serious golf circles. Walter Travis got into the design business with this treasure in 1900 and reminders of its timelessness are everywhere, starting at the first tee where a sundial suggests you should play your round in three hours. Francis Ouimet (above, holding trophy) won the US Amateur here in 1914 and while notoriety has rarely been fixed on Ekwanok since then, it remains a New England gem.

WETHERSFIELD COUNTRY CLUB, CONNECTICUT

• For 32 summers, this stately design, a short drive from Hartford, hosted a popular PGA Tour stop whose roster of winners includes luminaries such as (pictured above, left to right) Lee Trevino, Sam Snead, and Arnold Palmer. Though the Tour eventually outgrew this 6,568-yard layout, Wethersfield CC didn't lose a bit of respect. It features a marvelous double-green that is shared by the par-4 10th and par-3 13th.

wethersfield

Tiers of trouble

BRAD FAXON *typically needs no introduction in New England, and that's even truer in this case, given that he wrote the foreword on Page 8. The pride of Barrington, Rhode Island, Faxon was the natural choice to lead off the following series of picks with a gem from his longtime stomping ground.*

FAVORITE HOLE • Faxon loves playing golf in the state where he spent much of his childhood, so his pick is the par-3 17th at his home course, Rhode Island Country Club in Barrington. It plays from 120 to 145 yards.

WHAT MAKES IT FUN • "It's a classic Donald Ross design, a par 3 right on Narragansett Bay. The wind normally blows out of the southwest, off the water, making club selection very difficult. I have played anything from a wedge to a 5-iron. Once you get it on the green, the difficulty is not over because it's a two-tiered green."

HIS RECOMMENDATION • "Par is a good score, but missing the green will make par a tough task. Middle of the green always works on this hole."

18 great holes

A dream green

New Hampshire native **KIRK HANEFELD** *has captured multiple New England PGA Pro-Pro Match Play titles. Before serving as director of golf at The International in Bolton, Massachusetts, Hanefeld was director of golf at The Ridge Club in Sandwich and served for many years as the head pro at Salem Country Club in Peabody.*

FAVORITE HOLE · The par-4 13th at Salem CC. It plays to about 340 yards.

WHAT MAKES IT FUN · It proves that "a par 4 doesn't need to be long to be good." From the tee, a player looks out at a narrow fairway. "It has great bunkering on the right side and short of the green. The heathered hill on the left is beautiful and is a good tee-shot target. [Famed architect] Donald Ross was quoted as saying it was his best green design ever." The green slopes back to front and presents a multitude of devilish pin placements.

HIS RECOMMENDATION · Best to play a long iron or fairway wood into the valley, "which should set up a shot anywhere from 120 to 140 yards to a small, but extremely undulating green." Hanefeld says club selection is critical for the approach. Keep your ball below the hole for an uphill putt.

A creek runs through it

ANNE MARIE TOBIN *is one of the most accomplished players in New England golf history. She's won numerous Women's Golf Association of Massachusetts Championships, five of them in a row, and the organization's Player of the Year trophy is named in her honor. Her husband, Jim, is the head professional at Bellevue Golf Club in Melrose, Massachusetts.*

FAVORITE HOLE · The par-4 third at Bellevue GC, which plays anywhere from 320 to 403 yards. There's a creek that first appears about 100 yards off the tee, then runs through the woods laterally on the right and again crosses the fairway about 90 yards from the green. The hole is a dogleg right, with a large maple tree down the right side. "It overhangs the right side, which forces you to play to the left," said Tobin. "Otherwise, you will be blocked out and have to lay up short of the creek." The second shot is uphill, though you won't have a clear shot at the pin unless you hit a straight drive 210 to 220 yards for the women, 240 to 250 for the men.

WHAT MAKES IT FUN · "It takes four good shots to make par," said Tobin, "and there are three very different tees that can be used, each one changing the hole drastically."

HER RECOMMENDATION · "I like to play a draw to the middle of the fairway, keeping it away from the right side," said Tobin. The landing area is about 25 yards wide, but a good drive will leave you 160-180 yards in, depending upon conditions. Having done that, you take aim at a green that is protected on the right by a bunker and on the left by a slope that will kick everything down into trees. "And the green slopes away from you, so long and over the green is dead," said Tobin.

It's no breeze

DICK HASKELL, *who retired in 1998 after 30 years as executive director of the Massachusetts Golf Association, may be the best friend the tournament golfers of that state ever have had. Under his direction, the MGA expanded and enhanced its tournament schedule to the point where it is held in high esteem nationally.*

FAVORITE HOLE • The par-4 18th at Essex County Club in Manchester, Massachusetts. It plays 388 yards from the white tees, 408 from the blues, and is a par 5 of 410 yards for women.

WHAT MAKES IT FUN • "It's a very elevated tee with a panoramic view, an exciting finishing hole," said Haskell. "You get a personal satisfaction of playing it well. It's an easy hole to win [in match play], but an easy hole to lose."

HIS RECOMMENDATION • The tee shot means everything. Depending upon wind conditions — and judging the wind is the most difficult thing about this hole, because it swirls wildly — you'll need to drive it 200 to 220 yards. At that point, "you have hit the saddle," said Haskell, and the ball will roll down the slope, adding more distance — especially if Essex is in its vintage form of hard and fast. Mission accomplished? Not really, because even with just 140 yards left, the green is a difficult target. There's a brook in front, and the putting surface is small.

MARION MANEY MCINERNEY *has been one of the Bay State's most consistent female competitors over several decades. A highlight of her competitive career was the 1992 US Women's Mid-Amateur Championship, in which she defeated the legendary Carol Semple Thompson, 1 up, on the 19th hole of the final match at Old Marsh Golf Club in Palm Beach Gardens, Florida. A member at Charles River Country Club in Newton, Massachusetts, McInerney gets a steady diet of this classic Donald Ross layout. As for her favorite hole, it's an easy choice — she got engaged on this green.*

FAVORITE HOLE · The par-4 third hole at Charles River CC.

WHAT MAKES IT FUN · It's a splendid par 4, one that helps ease you into your round. It plays anywhere from 368 to 380 yards and demands a good tee shot. There is a group of trees down the left side and trees run all the way down the right, where out-of-bounds markers come into play for those who stray at this gentle dogleg left. The green is one of the few flat ones at Charles River, but devilish pin placements (particularly back left) are available, so beware.

HER RECOMMENDATION · "Play a slight draw off the tee, and be sure to use enough club to reach the green because it plays longer than you think."

Diamond in the rough

Water-view Cape

BOBBY ORR *revolutionized the game of hockey and provided two generations of Boston fans a display of grace and style that will never be seen again. Orr may rank even higher as a person. And if you were to poll local sports fans for their all-time athletic heroes, we'd wager No. 4 would rank No. 1. As for life after hockey, much of the competitive void has been filled by his love of golf.*

FAVORITE HOLE · The par-3 17th island green at The Ridge Club in Sandwich, Massachusetts, where Orr has a home and plays most of his golf. And for good reason — it's a marvelous course with tree-lined fairways and nice elevation changes. The hole plays from 80 to 150 yards.

WHAT MAKES IT FUN · "I look forward to the hole whenever I play a round," said Orr. "It's a huge green and you're only hitting an easy 8- or hard 9-iron, but you don't know which way the wind is blowing and it's all over water."

HIS RECOMMENDATION · Unless the wind is howling, Orr suggests an 8- or 9-iron and just aim for the center of the green. A back left pin is the toughest, and one you normally don't aim for.

So nice, play it twice

DICK STIMETS *was the consummate gentleman golfer, a lifelong amateur cut in the mold of Francis Ouimet, for whom he caddied. A member at Oyster Harbors in Osterville, Massachusetts, Stimets had a wall full of trophies for his golfing accomplishments, but his victory in the State Mid-Am at New Seabury in abysmal conditions is part of local folklore.*

FAVORITE HOLE · The dogleg right, par-4 ninth at Whitinsville Golf Club. Being a nine-hole course, you play it twice. As the ninth, it's 416 yards, 292 for women. As the 18th, it's a hefty 446 and a par 5 of 416 for women. You must carry water with your tee shot, but the water then runs down the right side, so you can be bold and try to cut off as much as you choose.

Beware: To really be aggressive down the right side requires a carry of 280 yards. The fairway slopes left to right, toward the water, and the green is small and undulated. From the white tees, a normal drive will leave you about 160-170 yards in; the second time around, the tee moves back and over, so the dogleg is more pronounced, and your approach shot will be closer to 200 yards.

WHAT MAKES IT FUN · "It is one of Donald Ross's great par 4s," said Stimets. "There is great length and it requires a precise second shot."

HIS RECOMMENDATION · Take aim off the tee at some small trees in the distance, middle left of the fairway. If you're too far right, your ball will kick toward the water. "It's a typical Ross green, so be accurate," said Stimets.

Drive time

CHARLIE VOLPONE *won the Massachusetts State Amateur in 1956 and the State Open in 1971, then paraded around New England to win state opens in New Hampshire, Maine, Vermont, and Rhode Island. He served as head pro at Nashawtuc Country Club in Concord, Massachusetts, for years, but then had his amateur status reinstated. He went on to become a two-time winner of the State Four-ball Championship, paired with Joe Keller, and later returned to the pro world.*

FAVORITE HOLE • The par-4 seventh at Concord Country Club. It plays anywhere from 290 to 345 yards. From the start on this course, you have a grueling stretch of par 4s, so when you get here you think you have a breather. "But many a player has met disaster here, assuming it was a breeze," said Volpone. There are trees down both sides and the fairway is narrow until it opens up if you drive dead straight for about 225 yards.

WHAT MAKES IT FUN • "It's an architect's challenge for strategy," said Volpone. "You can play it safe off the tee and have a difficult shot into the green, or play aggressively and have a short iron."

HIS RECOMMENDATION • The club of choice is driver. Always. That's because, "I'd rather hit a short iron into this green than a longer iron." Just don't be above the pin — and be careful about the small stream that guards the right side and has swallowed many safe iron tee shots.

Seaside splendor

BILL FOLEY, *the 1964 Massachusetts Amateur champion, has served as president of the Ouimet Scholarship Fund. Golf has been central to his life since his caddie days at the Wollaston Golf Club (then in Quincy, now in Milton, Massachusetts), where he eventually became a member. Foley served as president of the Massachusetts Golf Association and has worked as a rules official at both USGA and MGA events.*

FAVORITE HOLE · The par-3 third at Kittansett Club in Marion, Massachusetts. It plays anywhere from 120 to 165 yards and is the definition of a seaside hole. That's because when the tide is high, you have to hit over the water, and when it's out, you can easily land your shot on the beach.

WHAT MAKES IT FUN · "It's a beautiful view, with the sea, the wind, the sand," said Foley. And because it's difficult and comes early on, it has a tendency to get you emotionally charged for your round of golf.

HIS RECOMMENDATION · At all costs, "you need to strike a solid iron shot," said Foley. As for the club selection, who knows? It could be a 9-iron to a 3-iron, depending upon the wind, and if you hit it left-to-right, ease off because the beach is in play.

Eye on the ball

CAM NEELY, *once a hard-nosed, superstar right wing with the Boston Bruins, is now an avid golfer and fund-raiser for charitable causes.*

FAVORITE HOLE · The par-3 fourth at Farm Neck Golf Club on Martha's Vineyard in Massachusetts plays 116 to 175 yards from a slightly elevated tee to a smallish green that slopes left to right. But before you tee off, you have all you can do to keep your mind on your business. That's because the view is spectacular, with Sengekontacket Pond just beyond the green and Vineyard Sound in the background.

WHAT MAKES IT FUN · "It's a hole that can make or break your front-side score," said Neely. "Not an easy par 3." While it's a short club in, anything from a 7-iron to wedge, there's plenty of trouble.

HIS RECOMMENDATION · OK, the bad news, according to Neely: "Anything left is trouble, long is gone, and right is either unplayable or out of bounds" because of a marsh. If you are short, chances are you will be in the bunker, and don't expect to run it up, either. "It tends to be soft down there," said head professional Michael Zoll, "so you've got to find the green."

Dogleg day afternoon

A native of Portsmouth, New Hampshire, JANE BLALOCK *won 26 LPGA Tour events, the first at the Lady Carling in Atlanta in 1970, the last in 1985 at the Mazda Japan Classic. Before her pro career, she was a dynamic junior player — five times the New Hampshire State Amateur champ and twice the winner of the New England Amateur. She also was a standout player at Rollins College.*

FAVORITE HOLE · The par-4 ninth at The Ridge Club in Sandwich, Massachusetts — a dogleg left that plays from 312 to 415 yards. A bunker protects the left side of the fairway, and when you get to the green it is long and narrow. Pine trees dominate the right side of the fairway, and "it allows little room for error."

WHAT MAKES IT FUN · "It challenges you to carry the bunker [down the left], but encourages you to take the safer shot to the right-center of the fairway," said Blalock. In matches, she said, this hole is usually critical.

HER RECOMMENDATION · Play a slight draw off the tee, avoiding that bunker whatever you do. "That leaves you a mid-iron and if you have a little cutting action going," even better, she said. The green is well protected by bunkers, so if you don't hit the green, best be clear of the sand, which makes for a difficult finish.

MARY GALE

A job well done

MARY GALE *is a longtime standout on the Women's Golf Association of Massachusetts scene who won the association's stroke play championship in 1986 and match-play title in 1996.*

FAVORITE HOLE · The par-4 ninth at Tatnuck Country Club in Worcester, Massachusetts. It plays between 385 and 395 yards and is a favorite because it combines great design, aesthetics, and the inherent challenge of hitting two good shots. It is a slight dogleg right and the tee shot presents two immediate challenges — trees down the left and bunkers on the right. A drive down the right side makes it almost impossible to reach the green in two, and too far right spells trouble in the form of out-of-bounds.

WHAT MAKES IT FUN · Like any great hole, the ninth gives you a sense of accomplishment if you achieve par. Even after a good drive, you are faced with a downhill approach to a green that has a narrow opening with trees right and a pond left.

HER RECOMMENDATION · While the tee shot appears straightforward, it is best to be down the left side to get a clear shot at the green. A good tee shot allows you to reach with a 4- or 5-iron, though oftentimes you must take more club. The fairway slopes gently to the left, so take that into account as you hit your second shot. While the green is generally flat and rolls true, don't be greedy. Two putts for par is an accomplishment that provides a rewarding feeling as you leave the green.

No tee party

Longtime New England PGA standout PAUL BARKHOUSE *has a resume that includes State Open titles in Massachusetts, Maine, and New Hampshire, as well as a pair of NEPGA Senior Championships. He has shared victory in the NEPGA Pro-Pro Stroke Play Championship multiple times, including wins with Les Bond and Woburn Country Club colleague Paul Parajeckas.*

FAVORITE HOLE • The par-4 1st at Ferncroft Country Club in Danvers, Massachusetts. It plays between 342 and 401 yards and requires an accurate tee shot because of a large bunker left and a water hazard right.

WHAT MAKES IT FUN • It fulfills a requirement of mine for a good opening hole — that is, it is an accurate introduction of all the holes that are to follow," said Barkhouse, who was the head pro at Ferncroft for many years. Even after negotiating a good drive, your work isn't done, because the second shot is difficult. The small green is well bunkered and protected on the right by a large pine tree.

HIS RECOMMENDATION • Be prepared to start your round, because at Ferncroft you aren't provided a "whack away" mentality on the first tee. Focus on your tee shot, and on your approach; the correct club is essential.

Every last shot counts

GEOFF SISK *is a two-time State Open champ from Marshfield, Massachusetts, who played on the PGA Tour in 1999.*

FAVORITE HOLE · The par-4 18th at his home club, Marshfield Country Club. It plays as long as 406 yards, and the green is elevated. "It's fun because of the challenge," said Sisk. The first challenge is the drive, because the landing area is narrow, and "there is no letup after the tee shot." A large bunker guards the right front of the green, and there's another parallel to the left of the green.

WHAT MAKES IT FUN · "It's a great finishing hole. No lead is safe coming into the 18th," said Sisk.

HIS RECOMMENDATION · A well-struck tee shot will leave you 150 to 180 yards, but you're better off in the left-center of the fairway. Keep in mind that the green is undulating and sneaky fast, from back to front. Therefore, your approach must stay below the pin — and on the same side of the green. If it's Sunday, the pin will be back right, making you carry a bunker with your approach.

CY KILGORE *plays his golf out of Tedesco Country Club in Marblehead, Massachusetts, but his success has stretched to that popular vacation spot in the Atlantic where a couple of times he has won the Bermuda Amateur.*

FAVORITE HOLE · The par-5 15th that turns right all the way around a huge pond at Presidents Golf Course in Quincy, Massachusetts, a municipal course that hosts the annual Norfolk County Classic. Players stand on an extremely elevated tee and stare down at a narrow fairway with a bunker on the left and a huge pond on the right. The hole measures 435 to 500 yards, though that is measuring all the way around the pond; it plays much shorter if you take the direct route. "It may not be the prettiest hole we play," said Kilgore, "but it offers plenty of challenge."

WHAT MAKES IT FUN · "It's the best risk/reward par 5 we play in our state competition," said Kilgore. "Even the shortest hitter can reach it." Indeed, the charm of the hole is that with two solid hits, even mid- to high-handicappers can experience the glory of making an eagle putt, though to get there a golfer must fight off the nerves that come with a 170- to 190-yard shot over water.

HIS RECOMMENDATION · "Depending on the wind, it can be a [low] iron to a driver, taken at the bunker on the left. Now you have a shot anywhere from 200 to 170 yards over the water to a green that is protected on the left by a bunker and behind and to the right by another hazard." The prevailing wind is usually in your face, the green is notoriously firm, so you may choose to lay up. Fine, except "that's a difficult shot, too," said Kilgore. That's because you still have to deal with at least a corner of the pond, taking aim at a small, well-bunkered landing area.

Perched over a pond

Flourish at the finish

A PGA member since 1991, **SUSAN BOND** *is head professional at Weekapaug Golf Club in Westerly, Rhode Island.*

FAVORITE HOLE · The par-5 18th at Wellesley Country Club in Massachusetts. Her fondness for this closing hole comes as no surprise, given the ending to the 1993 Massachusetts Women's Open. Bond was tied with playing partner Michelle Dobek as they stood on the 18th tee in the final round. After each drove into the fairway, they were sent to the clubhouse to wait out an hour rain delay. When they returned, Bond sank a 5-foot birdie putt to prevail. The hole plays anywhere from 394 to 438 yards, though for top-level men's events — such as the State Open — it is played as a par 4.

WHAT MAKES IT FUN · Like most par 5s, it offers longer hitters the chance to reach in two, though most will try to reach in three. It is fairly straight, but an elevated green presents a serious challenge. The green is small, so as you walk off the 17th tee, you can look down and see where the pin placement is, an important piece of information because you don't want to go over this green.

HER RECOMMENDATION · For those playing it as a three-shotter, a safe drive would be followed by whatever club gets you to the base of the hill — anything from a 3-wood to a mid-iron.

Island of trouble

FRANK VANA JR. *of Boylston, Massachusetts, is a seven-time State Mid-Am champ and eight-time MGA Player of the Year.*

FAVORITE HOLE · The par-3 12th at Marlborough Country Club in Massachusetts, his home club. It plays between 145 and 165 yards and while it's not a pure island green, it plays like one. That's because there's a small brook that protects the front, left, and right, and though it doesn't stretch to the back of the green, that's not a bail-out area.

WHAT MAKES IT FUN · "Whether it's a casual round or a serious match, this tee shot never really leaves your mind until your ball is safely on the green," said Vana. Hitting from an elevated tee, you're facing a tee shot that can "make or break your round." The wind normally blows left to right, making the green seem even smaller. Once on the green, there are relatively few flat putts, said Vana. Most of the green slopes toward the middle, except for balls on the front left.

HIS RECOMMENDATION · "Take aim at the center of the green. That's the only place you should be trying to hit it," said Vana. "If you're in match play, hitting the green applies pressure if you go first; in stroke play, getting on in regulation seems to boost your confidence, settle your nerves, and allow the rest of the round to flow easier." Vana has seen many shots get swallowed up by the shallow brook, but warns against the strong temptation to play from the water. "That's a miracle shot," he said.

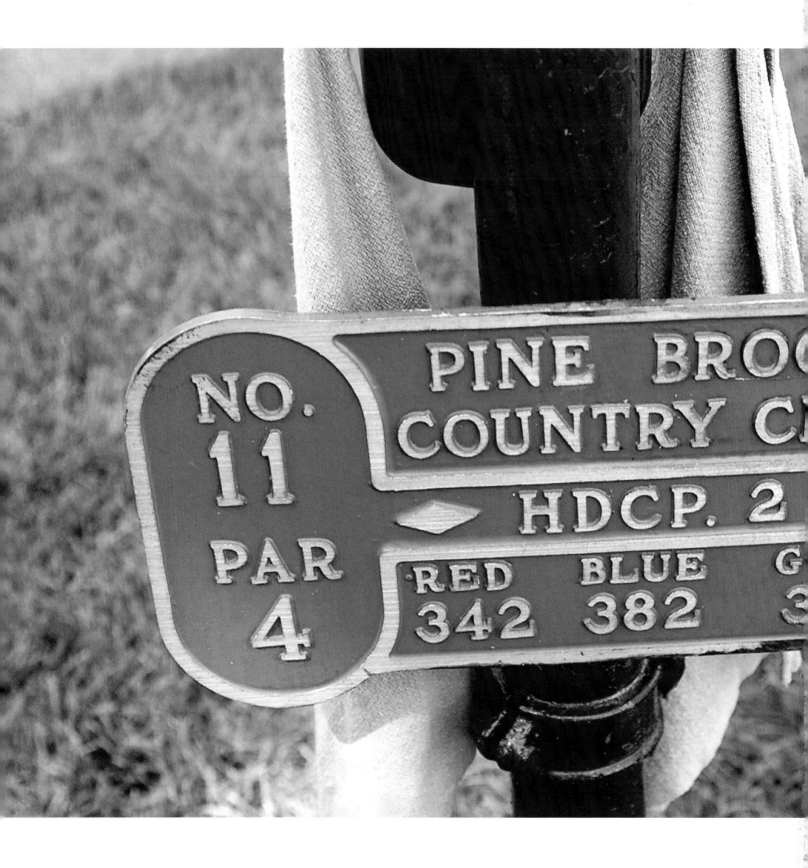

Old dog, new tricks

BOB CROWLEY *is known as much for his formidable playing skills as for his many decades at Pine Brook Country Club in Weston, Massachusetts. Five times he won the New England PGA Championship and he made the rounds in the state opens, winning Massachusetts, Maine, New Hampshire, and Vermont. There were also victories in the NEPGA Pro-Pro Stroke Play event, as well as NEPGA Senior Championships.*

FAVORITE HOLE · The par-4 11th at Pine Brook, the definitive risk/reward hole. It doglegs left at 45 degrees and plays anywhere from 342 to 387 yards. Once you get around the corner, the last 110 yards or so are uphill to a well-bunkered green. There is out-of-bounds left and the putting surface is a difficult one.

WHAT MAKES IT FUN · It presents a challenge if you play aggressively, but it also offers a distinct method of attack for the player choosing to be conservative. And although great emphasis is on the tee shot, the approach is formidable, with anything short likely to roll back into the fairway.

HIS RECOMMENDATION · "There are three or four ways to play it," said Crowley, starting with the most conser-vative approach: the medium iron to a safe part of the fairway that leaves you a long iron in. From there, your choices increase in aggressiveness, because you can take a longer iron off the tee and whip it around the corner to set up a midiron approach, or you can get bold and hit a wood off the tee to give yourself a short iron in. Then there's the truly daring play: a driver up and over the corner, with a hook to set up a wedge second shot. But beware those of you hitting driver, because if you don't hook it, good luck.

it happened here

from the start, New England served as a logical launching pad for the introduction of golf to America.

Consider, first of all, who was doing the introductions: Scotsmen, for the most part. Their boat trips across the Atlantic would most conveniently arrive in Boston, bringing them from Dornoch and Glasgow, Edinburgh and St. Andrews. The names on board included Willie Campbell, Donald Ross, Robert White, and Dave Brown. These men knew how to play the game, but more than that, they knew how to teach others to play, and how to build and maintain the courses they created.

Consider, too, the makeup of Boston in the late 1800s and early 1900s: Brahmins and old Yankees. A good portion of these folks were of comfortable wealth, which is the slice of the populace who played golf and helped build courses in those years. Members of The Country Club in Brookline, Massachusetts, were among representatives from five clubs throughout the country who convened in 1895 to establish the United States Golf Association.

National championships got their start in New England (the first US Amateur and first US Open were run back-to-back at Newport Country Club in Rhode Island in 1895) and the region's embrace of the game has never waned. Through 2006, Massachusetts had played host to 52 USGA events, surpassed only by Pennsylvania (75), California (64), New York (64), and Illinois (55). Some 74 national championships have been contested in five of six New England states (only New Hampshire has not hosted) and when you add in two PGA Championships, several dozen PGA Tour and LPGA Tour events, and the unforgettable 1999 Ryder Cup, this area of the country has been blessed with distinguished golf tournaments for nearly 100 years.

One could argue that the first important visit was made in 1900, when Englishman Harry Vardon, the great British Open champion, put on an exhibition at a department store in downtown Boston and played matches throughout New England and the US. There's been a steady march of notable names and tournaments ever since. —J.M.

AMERICA'S FIRST SHOCKER

September 23, 1999

By JOE CONCANNON

As a lad growing up on Clyde Street in Brookline, Massachusetts, Francis Ouimet would frequently cut through swatches of The Country Club as he walked to and from the Putterham School. "Not that I was granted any such privileges," wrote Ouimet in his autobiography. "But in the role of trespasser I discovered that this route saved many footsteps, got me to school on time and, more important, enabled me to get home with the least possible delay."

There is no specific mention of the now-famous 17th hole at TCC, the Vardon trap that still cuts menacingly out into the fairway, or how a shot by Harry Vardon and a dramatic putt by Ouimet transformed the game as we knew it in America. When Vardon's attempt to cut the corner ended up against an embankment in the trap and Ouimet decisively holed his putt for a birdie, he led one of the giants of golf by three strokes with one hole left in a playoff for the 1913 US Open championship.

Ouimet was the neighborhood kid who picked up golf balls in his traipses over the hallowed turf of The Country Club and took to the game with a makeshift set of clubs. He was just 20, an amateur who had won the Massachusetts state championship earlier in the summer. He entered the US Open almost as an afterthought, qualified, and found himself tied with Vardon and fellow Briton Ted Ray entering the fourth round. The kid against the legends.

As the round evolved, Ouimet would falter against his adversaries, who were on an extended exhibition tour of the United States. It was the year before Vardon would win his record-sixth British Open, and World War I would lead to the suspension of championship golf in Europe. Ouimet needed to play the final two holes in 1 under to reach the historic playoff. So he walked to the 17th tee.

"A drive and a second shot placed my ball on the green 15 feet from the cup," wrote Ouimet. "It was now or never. ... I struck that putt as firmly as any putt I ever hit, saw it take a roll, bang smack against the back of the hole and fall in for the three."

After Ouimet managed to save par from the rough at 18, the playoff was on for Saturday.

Ray would fade out of serious contention on the 15th, when he took a six, and finish with a 78. Vardon trailed by one approaching the 17th tee, but took a bogey 5. When Ouimet holed his putt from 15 feet he was three clear.

"The 18th hole was a hard two-shotter," wrote Ouimet. "The rains had turned the race track in front of the green into a bog, and my one thought was to get over mud. All hit fine tee shots; I placed my second on the green. It did not enter my head that I was about to become the open champion until I stroked my first putt to within eight or nine inches of the hole. Then, as I stepped up to make that short putt, I became very nervous. I dropped the putt. Nothing but the most intense concentration brought me victory."

Vardon (77) would finish 5-6, so Ouimet, with his 3-4 finish, shot 72 to win by five strokes. This was acclaimed by headlines on both sides of the pond and, as the fabled British journalist Bernard Darwin once noted, Ouimet "laid, if I may respectfully say so, the foundation of the great American golfing empire." ⛳

FRANCIS OUIMET (holding horseshoe) is hoisted by fans after his unlikely triumph in a 1913 playoff caddied by 10-year-old Eddie Lowery (with towel).

ARNOLD PALMER (right) is beaten by a tree stump and a smoking Julius Boros (far right).

64

STUMPED IN BROOKLINE

September 23, 1999 • By JIM McCABE

The June chill was still in the air, the wet grass was locking onto any club, and with every swing, this monster of a course kept getting bigger.

Time was running out; the deficit, a manageable two shots just a few holes ago, was now four. Arnold Palmer could swing hard and try to make something happen, but he always did that. No, now was the time to swing really hard.

The 12th hole was where he could jump back into this 1963 US Open at The Country Club in Brookline, Massachusetts. Palmer had deemed that section of the course "ridiculous" earlier in the week, and he was sure he wasn't off base. The hole ran some 300 yards straight out from the tee and then sharply rose uphill for another 160 yards of fairway.

Still, Palmer had birdied that hole twice and if he could do it again, this playoff could swing in his favor. The thought kick-started his engine, at least for a moment, and he forgot his stomach was twisting. What was it that he ate last night?

The intestinal problem had plagued him all day, but Palmer tried to ignore it. He also attempted to forget about the big move he was going to make at the 12th and take care of a more pressing matter — the 11th hole.

It wasn't as hard as 12, thought Palmer. "So why am I playing so poorly?" There had been a pair of routine pars in rounds 1 and 2, then a triple, then a bogey. Palmer hitched at his belt, pulled up his pants, and thought to himself, "Time for a birdie."

Then, thwaaaccckkk ... the swing was over in the blink of an eye, his rapid takeaway matched only by the ferocious follow-through. His driver shot skyward, and as usual, Palmer was twisted in a knot to follow the flight of his tee ball. But the forehead was wrinkled. The scowl was on. So was the hook.

It was headed left, in a hurry. Palmer's quickly realized the ball had not reached the corner and he would be blocked out. So he started on one of the longest and loneliest walks a golfer can make — to a ball in trouble — and he found the ball resting in a rotted tree stump.

Palmer stared at his ball and considered taking a drop. "How can I? I'm already down five shots," he said to himself. A quick glance up brought 43-year-old, Connecticut-native Julius Boros into view. The man with the lead had one (1952) US Open title under his belt and had already made three birdies on the day. "He's sitting dead middle of the fairway; I'm over here in a tree stump, and I'm going to take a drop? No chance," thought Palmer.

On the other side of Boros was Jacky Cupit. The young, unheralded Texan could have won this tournament in regulation, but a double bogey at the 17th proved costly. Now, he, too, was trying to mount a charge from a very difficult situation. He was buried in thick rough, probably unable to get it safely home in two, and he waited for Palmer to punch out.

Only Palmer was not going to punch out.

"You've got to be kidding," Cupit whispered to himself. "What is he doing?"

Palmer wasn't quite sure, but he knew he wasn't going to surrender any more shots without a fight, and the sleeves were certainly rolled up now as he took a full swing with a long iron. He had to come down at a steep angle, catch the ball cleanly, and rip through it because the wood was certainly tougher than turf.

Spectators formed a semicircle and tried to lean closer. The club shot straight up, then Palmer dropped the hammer quickly, only the club face caught too much of the trunk and even he, with all his forearm strength, couldn't get to the ball.

The club bounced. Palmer had completely missed.

The blood started boiling.

With little set-up he swung the club again, this time taking it back faster, following through even quicker.

Thump.

Again he hit the tree stump. Again the club bounced. Again he missed the ball.

The 1963 US Open was now over, at least for him.

Finally, with another swing at it, Palmer was able to move the ball back onto the fairway. He looked toward Boros, who had drilled a 3-iron to 12 feet and silently acknowledged that the chase was done.

In the end, Boros shot 70, Cupit 73, Palmer 76. But it was the 11th hole itself that stole the show.

"The Boston Tree Stump," said Palmer many years later when asked about the '63 Open. "I remember." ⚲

THE MOTHER OF ALL RYDERS

September 22, 1999 • By JIM McCABE

There are pictures and framed letters to remind guests that they have walked into a cherished Massachusetts home of yesteryear. Clocks can be found, if you need to have the day's time, but calendars are not required. At Worcester Country Club, it can be any year your imagination desires, for a century's worth of character, charm, and elegance is beneath every step taken on the golf course and behind every door of the clubhouse.

Donald Ross created this marvelous golf course, which has been preserved by grateful guardians, and there are still some who may have been there that September day in 1914 when President William H. Taft struck the first drive. It was here, in 1925, that golf's greatest legend, Robert Tyre Jones Jr., contributed the most gracious act of sportsmanship the game has ever seen. Fourteen years later, Byron Nelson won a Mass. Open on these hallowed grounds.

Then there were those gentlemen who arrived in early June of 1927. A proud group of Brits, they had taken a ship, the Aquitania, across the Atlantic, disembarking in Manhattan. A few days later, following a look at Babe Ruth and the Yankees and some golf in Westchester, the men found themselves in the rolling hills of central Massachusetts.

They had come to play golf for honor. They had come to play golf for pride. They had come to play the first official Ryder Cup Matches.

At Worcester Country Club? Why Worcester?

It isn't documented, but the reason seems to be threefold.

Most likely, the players agreed on Worcester CC since many of them had taken part in the US Open there two years earlier. (That was the Open in which Jones called a penalty stroke on himself and was forced into a playoff, which he lost to Willie MacFarlane.)

Logistically, Worcester made sense because the US Open would be held two weeks later at Oakmont in

THE VICTORIOUS 1927 US TEAM included (front, l-r) Leo Diegel, Bill Mehlhorn, Walter Hagen, Al Espinosa, Gene Sarazen, (rear, l-r) Johnny Golden, Joe Turnesa, Johnny Farrell, and Al Waltrous. **FRED HILL** (right) caddied for Sarazen.

Pennsylvania, and the Brits could use the matches as a warmup.

Finally, Worcester's head professional at the time was Willie Ogg, a legendary figure. He was a Scotsman who was friendly with many of the Brits, while also involved with the PGA of America. It stands to reason that he had an influence on the decision to bring this international golf match to Worcester.

But whatever got them to Worcester serves as trivial backdrop to the reality that indeed, on June 3-4, 1927, a golf competition was born in Massachusetts. Eighteen professional golfers with their fashionable knickers and ties, their mashies and niblicks, their loose swings and combative spirits

started something that they could not recognize if they were with us today.

None of them are, of course, not with the 1999 passing of Gene Sarazen at the age of 97. He had been the last remaining player from that 1927 competition. "A wonderful man," recalled Fred Hill. "He was a little nervous, a bit cocky, but he was very generous."

Hill caddied for Sarazen in 1927 and received $80. The money he gave to his mother; the memories he still has.

It would be exaggerating to say the first Ryder Cup match dominated news. Not with the country still trumpeting Charles Lindbergh's historic flight while also monitoring the plight of Clarence Chamberlin, lost in

travel. There was also the death of the infamous Lizzie Borden. Charlie Chaplin had himself in a marital mess, and the Sacco-Vanzetti case was a hot topic of conversation.

Still, golf was a pleasant enough distraction. The Americans, humbled terribly by a 13 ½-1 ½ score in an informal match the year before at Gleneagles in Scotland, won three of four foursomes matches on Friday. The next day, despite the cool, damp, and windy weather that seemed to make the Brits feel right at home, the Homebreds — as they had come to be called in America — won six of eight singles matches, halved another, and completed a memorable 9 ½-2 ½ victory. ⚑

ANOTHER RYDER TO REMEMBER

September 24, 2002 • By JIM McCABE

The crowds have all gone and the grass has come back. It is beautiful green grass, an emerald floor beneath tall, waving trees that have stood for decades. The trees help protect a solitude that is cherished at The Country Club, but for three fall days in 1999, they acted as tunnel walls for a surge of noise that shook the hallowed ground in Brookline, Massachusetts, like never before.

Perhaps you were there. If you weren't, most likely you know someone who was, for the 33rd Ryder Cup was a spectacle to be seen, to be experienced, to be felt, and by the tens of thousands they came. Normally a private enclave, The Country Club provided the stage for a public unveiling of golf history from Sept. 24-26, 1999. And, as they are bound to do, some critics have weighed in with a historical perspective that isn't always flattering. To some, the competition was too contentious, the crowd too vocal, the entire affair too big.

But ask them about the golf.

The golf?

Yes, the golf. The reason the event was held in the first place.

They'll concede it was remarkable: flat-out brilliant at times, thrilling and jam-packed with highlights. No complaints with the level of play, or with the passion with which the matches were contested. None at all.

He has heard all the complaints, but what still echoes in John Cornish's ears is something he heard at the first tee that crisp, cool, beautiful Sunday morning just before the singles competition got under way.

"Tom Lehman and Lee Westwood were about to play, and all of a sudden the crowd started singing the national anthem," said Cornish, who was chairman of TCC's Ryder Cup Committee. "It was spontaneous, and then Lehman was leading the crowd. You kind of knew right there that something special was going to happen."

Of course, something special did unfold that day. Criticism of rowdy spectators and an infamous celebration on the 17th green aside, it was a sporting event for the ages.

The golfing highlights were many, but perhaps no sequence was as enthralling as the Friday afternoon four-ball. Trailing, 2 ½-1 ½, after the morning foursomes, the US hoped to rejuvenate its cause in a format that usually lends itself to great scoring.

How good was it? Take the first match, Sergio Garcia and Jesper Parnevik vs. Phil Mickelson and Jim Furyk. They combined to birdie 13 of the first 14 holes, four times matching birdies. Parnevik holed out a 9-iron from just inside of 150 yards at the par-4 eighth for an eagle. Then, with the match tied, Garcia knew Mickelson had a 4-footer for birdie at the 534-yard, par-5 14th when he pitched in for an eagle to highlight a 1-up win.

Good stuff, but at that same 14th hole minutes later, Paul Lawrie rolled in about a 30-footer for eagle, seemingly putting him and Colin Montgomerie 1 up. But Davis Love responded by sinking his own 25-foot eagle putt, and when he made another clutch putt at the 18th, the Love-Justin Leonard tandem had earned a halve.

It only got better, because Darren Clarke made seven birdies, including one at the 17th to go 1 up, to help him and Westwood beat Tiger Woods and David Duval in the first day's final match.

On and on went the weekend highlights: Garcia chipping in from 50 yards at the par-4 12th to team with Parnevik in a 3-and-2 win over Leonard and Payne Stewart ... Love nearly making a double eagle, hitting a sensational second shot into the par-5 ninth green from an elevated cliff right of the fairway ... Leonard and Hal Sutton going bogey-free in a four-ball halve with Jose Maria Olazabal and Miguel Angel Jimenez ... Woods and Steve Pate with birdies on the first four holes, then an eagle on the 14th to beat Jimenez and Padraig Harrington in foursomes ... Sutton and Jeff Maggert birdieing three of the final four holes to sneak past Montgomerie and Lawrie, who birdied two of those last four holes.

Through it all, the roars grew louder, and the grounds came alive with excitement.

"I wasn't there that day at Augusta [in 1986] when Jack Nicklaus shot 30 on the back [for a stunning come-from-behind win], but I can imagine that's how it sounded, with the cheers reverberating," said Cornish.

Cornish had probably wondered on several occasions whether it was worth getting involved in the event, but when he got to the first tee Sunday and heard the national anthem, when he watched Lehman dismantle Westwood and ignite wins in the first six matches, when he witnessed an American team pull together in unprecedented fashion, he knew he had made the right decision.

The Country Club had played host to the event of a lifetime. ⚑

1954
US Women's
Open

BABE DIDRIKSON ZAHARIAS

BEWITCHED BY BABE

June 27, 2004 · By JIM McCABE

It's a golf achievement so grand that it ranks right up there with the best of them: In 1954, one Mildred "Babe" Didrikson Zaharias stormed to victory in the US Women's Open at Salem Country Club in Peabody, Massachusetts.

Consider that it was her third triumph in five starts in that major event. Take into account that she won it by an incredible 12 shots, a margin that is second largest in tournament history. Throw in that she has long stood as the oldest winner, at 43. Put it all together and you get a pretty impressive performance.

Then digest this: The woman was ravaged with cancer at the time.

"My goodness, it was pure guts at Salem," said LPGA Tour legend Louise Suggs. "She had game, sure, but you could just feel it: her determination to win that tournament. And she did."

Suggs is a big reason there is an LPGA Tour and a US Women's Open, but she was never president of the Babe Zaharias Fan Club. They were founding members of the LPGA Tour and they were fierce competitors who had mutual respect, but the Babe loved the spotlight, sought it out, and that rubbed some colleagues the wrong way.

"She'd say, 'If you don't have me, you don't have a tournament,' and in a lot of ways, she was right," said Suggs. "But I reminded her that she needed other players, too."

Still, Zaharias's 1954 performance may live forever as the ultimate one-person show. She had been diagnosed with colon cancer in the spring of 1953, sat out that entire season, yet came back in '54 to win twice early.

Winners of US Golf Association events held in New England

US OPEN
1895 · **Horace Rawlins** · Newport CC, RHODE ISLAND
1898 · **Fred Herd** · Myopia Hunt Club, MASSACHUSETTS
1901 · **Willie Anderson** · Myopia Hunt Club, MASSACHUSETTS
1905 · **Willie Anderson** · Myopia Hunt Club, MASSACHUSETTS
1908 · **Fred McLeod** · Myopia Hunt Club, MASSACHUSETTS
1913 · **Francis Ouimet** · The Country Club, MASSACHUSETTS
1919 · **Walter Hagen** · Brae Burn CC, MASSACHUSETTS
1925 · **William Macfarlane** · Worcester CC, MASSACHUSETTS
1963 · **Julius Boros** · The Country Club, MASSACHUSETTS
1988 · **Curtis Strange** · The Country Club, MASSACHUSETTS

US WOMEN'S OPEN
1954 · **Babe Didrikson Zaharias** · Salem CC, MASSACHUSETTS
1960 · **Betsy Rawls** · Worcester CC, MASSACHUSETTS
1979 · **Jerilyn Britz** · Brooklawn CC, CONNECTICUT
1984 · **Hollis Stacy** · Salem CC, MASSACHUSETTS
2004 · **Meg Mallon** · The Orchards, MASSACHUSETTS
2006 · **Annika Sorenstam** · Newport CC, RHODE ISLAND

US SENIOR OPEN
1987 · **Gary Player** · Brooklawn CC, CONNECTICUT
2001 · **Bruce Fleisher** · Salem CC, MASSACHUSETTS

US AMATEUR PUBLIC LINKS
1978 · **Dean Prince** · Bangor Municipal, MAINE
1995 · **Chris Wollmann** · Stow Acres, MASSACHUSETTS

US GIRLS' JUNIOR
1953 · **Mildred Meyerson** · The Country Club, MASSACHUSETTS
1958 · **Judy Eller** · Greenwich CC, CONNECTICUT
1975 · **Dayna Benson** · Dedham Country & Polo, MASSACHUSETTS
1987 · **Michelle McGann** · The Orchards, MASSACHUSETTS
1995 · **Marcy Newton** · Longmeadow CC, MASSACHUSETTS
2003 · **Sukjin-Lee Wuesthoff** · Brooklawn CC, CONNECTICUT

US JUNIOR AMATEUR
1952 · **Donald Bisplinghoff** · Yale University GC, CONNECTICUT
1956 · **Harlan Stevenson** · Taconic GC, MASSACHUSETTS
1968 · **Eddie Pearce** · The Country Club, MASSACHUSETTS
1974 · **David Nevatt** · Brooklawn CC, CONNECTICUT
1988 · **Jason Widener** · Yale University GC, CONNECTICUT
1992 · **Tiger Woods** · Wollaston GC, MASSACHUSETTS
2005 · **Kevin Tway** · Longmeadow CC, MASSACHUSETTS

US WOMEN'S AMATEUR
1897 • **Beatrix Hoyt** • Essex CC, MASSACHUSETTS
1902 • **Genevieve Hecker** • The Country Club, MASSACHUSETTS
1906 • **Hariot Curtis** • Brae Burn CC, MASSACHUSETTS
1912 • **Margaret Curtis** • Essex CC, MASSACHUSETTS
1916 • **Alexa Stirling** • Belmont Springs, MASSACHUSETTS
1924 • **Dorothy Campbell Hurd** • Rhode Island CC, RHODE ISLAND
1932 • **Virginia Van Wie** • Salem CC, MASSACHUSETTS
1939 • **Betty Jameson** • Wee Burn CC, CONNECTICUT
1941 • **Elizabeth Hicks** • The Country Club, MASSACHUSETTS
1953 • **Mary Lena Faulk** • Rhode Island CC, RHODE ISLAND
1958 • **Anne Quast** • Wee Burn CC, CONNECTICUT
1963 • **Anne Quast Sander** • Taconic GC, MASSACHUSETTS
1970 • **Martha Wilkinson** • Wee Burn CC, CONNECTICUT
1975 • **Beth Daniel** • Brae Burn CC, MASSACHUSETTS
1987 • **Kay Cockerill** • Rhode Island CC, RHODE ISLAND
1995 • **Kelli Kuehne** • The Country Club, MASSACHUSETTS
1997 • **Silvia Cavalleri** • Brae Burn CC, MASSACHUSETTS

US AMATEUR
1895 • **Charles B. Macdonald** • Newport CC, RHODE ISLAND
1910 • **William Fownes** • The Country Club, MASSACHUSETTS
1914 • **Francis Ouimet** • Ekwanok CC, VERMONT
1922 • **Jess Sweetser** • The Country Club, MASSACHUSETTS
1928 • **Bobby Jones** • Brae Burn CC, MASSACHUSETTS
1934 • **Lawson Little** • The Country Club, MASSACHUSETTS
1957 • **Hillman Robbins** • The Country Club, MASSACHUSETTS
1982 • **Jay Sigel** • The Country Club, MASSACHUSETTS
1995 • **Tiger Woods** • Newport CC, RHODE ISLAND

US WOMEN'S MID-AMATEUR
1995 • **Ellen Port** • Essex CC, MASSACHUSETTS

US MID-AMATEUR
1996 • **John Miller** • Hartford GC, CONNECTICUT
2002 • **George Zahringer** • Stanwich Club, CONNECTICUT

US SENIOR AMATEUR
1960 • **Michael Cestone** • Oyster Harbors, MASSACHUSETTS
1977 • **Dale Morey** • Salem CC, MASSACHUSETTS
1996 • **O. Gordon Brewer** • Taconic GC, MASSACHUSETTS

Doctors never told her that the cancer had spread to her lymph nodes, so Zaharias was not aware of the severity of her situation when she opened with a 72 at Salem to share the first-round lead. When she followed with a 71, she had a seven-shot cushion over Betsy Rawls and the rout was on.

The performance is appreciated by golf historians, of course, but even more so by witnesses. And if those witnesses were in the field alongside Zaharias, well ... it's a memory that Joanne Goodwin and Geneo McAuliffe cherish.

"I remember being in the group behind her and how the fans could just walk in behind the players. There were a lot people following her and it was exciting to be there," said Goodwin, whose home course is Haverhill Country Club.

In 1954, Goodwin was an 18-year-old who had just won the state amateur championship. To be in the national championship alongside Zaharias, Rawls, Suggs, and Patty Berg? As a teenager? Goodwin was overwhelmed.

"I was so nervous, I was standing on the first tee, which was elevated, and my knees were shaking," she said. "I nearly topped the ball."

Playing in that 1954 Open, no matter how many shots Goodwin finished out of the lead, remains a coveted memory because it was the one in which the Babe became immortalized.

"I remember the 18th hole, how she hit it down there so far she had just a flip wedge into the green," said McAuliffe, who plays out of Woods Hole now but played out of Charles River back then. "I tell you, she could really hit the ball."

Zaharias played very little after that Open, which was probably the definitive performance in her career. She was hospitalized for most of 1955 and died September 27, 1956. ♀

MEG MALLON
hugs her trophy
(above) after out-
lasting Annika
Sorenstam (right)
and some soggy
weather (page 78)
to start off the
tournament.

59TH U.S. WOMEN'S C

HOLE	1	2	3	4	5	6	7
...ERS PAR	4	4	5	4	3	4	3
...CICOME *							
...EBOUC							
...RENSTAM A *							
...NIEL B	2	0	0	1	1		
...K *							
...SKE	0	0	1	1	1	1	
...SALES *							
...UMANN *							
...CH *							
...RST	0	1	0	0	0	0	0

2004 US Open

76

OLDEST WINNERS

In 2004, Meg Mallon became only the fourth golfer
in her 40s to win the US Women's Open:

YEAR	AGE
1954........*Babe Zaharias* • 43 years 7 days
2002........*Juli Inkster* • 42 years 13 days
2004........*Meg Mallon* • 41 years 2 months 20 days
1955........*Fay Crocker* • 40 years 11 months

MEG OVER ANNIKA

July 5, 2004 • By JIM McCABE

K.C. Jones, the Celtic legend and Hall of Famer, spotted talent in the kid when she was just 12 years old. It was the day she walked up to him and said, "Do you want to play golf? Because I can beat you."

"Think I was just a little precocious?" asked Meg Mallon.

Maybe then, but certainly not after the final round of the 59th US Women's Open when, for more than four hours, she walked beneath sizzling sunshine and into golf's record books. Saturated in charm and showcased on miles of a velvet green stage called The Orchards Golf Club of South Hadley, Massachusetts, Mallon hardly looked precocious; flawless is more like it.

Undaunted by a sterling performance by Annika Sorenstam just in front of her, Mallon played a round for the ages. Starting the day three behind Jennifer Rosales, Mallon shot a bogey-free, 6-under-par 65 — the lowest fourth-round score by a winner in this event — and stormed to a two-shot victory over Sorenstam, who finished birdie-birdie for a sparkling 67.

In reaching 10-under 274, Mallon claimed her second US Women's Open title and fourth career major, took home a check for $560,000, and left tens of thousands of people screaming in delight for what could be loosely called a homecoming — Mallon is Massachusetts-born and widely adored.

"It just felt right for me this week," said Mallon, who was born in Natick, though she lived there for just under a year. "I just love the culture here and in New England."

Whatever her inspiration, she turned in one of the greatest closing performances in the history of major championship golf. Maybe it wasn't as low as Johnny Miller's 63 to win the US Open at Oakmont in 1973, but Mallon truly authored a memorable performance, though it was hardly without a supporting cast.

There was, first and foremost, the painful meltdown by Rosales. So superb in getting to 7 under through three rounds and in possession of a three-shot cushion on Mallon, Sorenstam, and Kelly Robbins, the native of Manila made her only birdie of the day at the opening hole to go up by four, then slowly disintegrated on a blistering hot day. She shot 75-281 and was fourth.

Bogeys at the par-3 seventh and par-4 eighth sent her to the turn in 37, trailing by one to Mallon, who had birdied the par-5 third, par-4 fourth with a 54-foot cross-country putt, and par-5 ninth to go out in 33.

"I'm beside myself," said Mallon. "I haven't putted like this in so long."

Back in 1995, she had a three-shot lead in the US Women's Open and squandered it, losing out to a young Swede named Annika Sorenstam. "I was fully disgusted with myself at that performance," said Mallon, but her father said it was all right.

"I've always told her that you gave Annika her start in golf," said John Mallon. Then, pausing to digest what he had just watched on TV, he added: "What comes around, goes around, I guess."

That's because this time, Mallon didn't melt against Sorenstam, who was seeking her third US Women's Open title.

"I'm hoping she's feeling like she got beat today and didn't lose," said Mallon. Sorenstam agreed.

"To shoot 6 under on Sunday of the US Open is as good as it gets," said Sorenstam, a runner-up for the second time in three years.

Indeed, Mallon flat-out won with a performance that ranks with the best. Consider:

⌐ She played the last 25 holes without a bogey. What's more, after bogeying two of the first three holes Thursday, she made just four over the next 69.

⌐ At the most difficult three-hole stretch — the par-4 16th, par-3 17th, and par-4 18th — she went bogey-free and 2 under for four days.

⌐ On small, sloping greens, she didn't have one three-putt, and she put up an amazing 28 one-putts.

Even when the final bit of pressure was applied — Sorenstam making birdies at the 17th and 18th to close within two — Mallon showed her grit. She used an umbrella to get away from the sizzling sun, but gladly faced the heat thrown at her by Sorenstam. Mallon hit her best shot of the day — an 11-wood into the 178-yard 17th — and two-putted for par, then she went fairway, green, two putts at the 412-yard 18th to seal the win.

The family celebration was on — two brothers and two sisters in attendance — and another story involving a basketball legend was recalled.

"I wish I had a dime for every time a father told me he had a kid with talent," former Celtic Bob Cousy, a close friend of the Mallons, once said. "Except for John Mallon. He was the only one who was right." ⚲

A LONG STRANGE TRIP

June 21, 1988 • By JOE CONCANNON

Curtis Strange approached the 18th green of The Country Club in Brookline, Massachusetts, with the championship of the 88th US Open in hand. As he headed toward the grandstands that were overflowing with people, he thought of his late father and his days as a kid spent on the golf course in Virginia hitting shots by himself and waiting to be driven home.

"This is for my dad, " he would say later, as the emotion within welled up one more time. "I've been waiting a long time to do this, and I screwed up the 1985 Masters. I've been waiting a long time. I just had to thank the people somehow who gave [me] the opportunity. This is the greatest feeling I've ever had."

Strange honed the game he brought to this 1988 championship in the Tidewater region of Virginia under the watchful eye of his father, Tom, who died in 1969 when Curtis and twin brother Allen were 14. "My dad started me when I was 9 years old," the champion remembered. "I went around the golf course with him, and I learned the mechanics of the game from him. I just wish he could have been here."

Strange beat Great Britain's Nick Faldo by four shots in the championship's 28th playoff. He fired a level-par round of 71 on a sultry afternoon before a crowd that topped 20,000 and lined every fairway from tee to green in an outpouring of humanity that showed the world just how popular golf is in this part of the globe.

The victory gave Strange his first major championship ever, following two victories within the previous two months on the PGA Tour, and it merely solidified his position as one of the world's best players. He had let the Masters get away three years earlier when he hit shots into the water on the 13th and 15th holes, and he had no intention of letting this one get away at this stage of his career.

He beat British Open champion Faldo with a resolute exhibition of golf that included 11 one-putt greens during a round in which he hit just eight of 15 fairways. "What made it seem sloppy was the wind," said Strange. "The wind was tough to judge. Playoffs are tough. Sometimes you've got to reach down a little deeper."

The drama was played out in front of the huge crowds who decided to take a Monday off from whatever else they had to do. They spent it on this historic Brookline course where New Englanders had won two previous Open playoffs: The neighborhood kid from Clyde Street, Francis Ouimet, beat Britons Harry Vardon and Ted Ray in 1913, and Connecticut native Julius Boros beat Arnold Palmer and Jacky Cupit in 1963. This time, fans came to watch a golfer out of the colony of Virginia beat an Englishman from Surrey on a steaming June day in the suburbs of Boston. And it didn't hurt that the winner's caddie was a 32-year-old from Glastonbury, Connecticut: Greg Rita.

Faldo, who earned his ticket to the playoff when Strange three-putted the 17th in the final round of regulation, never led in what came down to a match-play competition. The last time they were tied was when Strange bogeyed the fourth hole, out of a trap behind the green. Strange took the lead he never surrendered on the fifth, when he followed his 8-iron second shot with a 10-foot birdie putt.

There was still an element of doubt through the 17th green, where it was Faldo's turn to undo himself when his 6-iron second shot bounded over the green and he was unable to get up and down. Strange's 7-iron second shot strayed into the right-side bunker but he exploded to within 4 feet and made the putt this time to take a three-shot cushion to the 18th tee.

"I knew I had it won," said Strange. "There's nothing like coming up the last hole with a three shot lead in a major."

"What can I say?" said Faldo. "I played well but didn't hole a few putts at the right time. ... I never put enough pressure on him."

Strange pocketed a $180,000 prize and the most important victory of his career. "It got me to that next level," said Strange. "It means what every little boy dreams about ... It means all the effort and all the work has paid off."

The Masters could be put to rest. The Sunday-afternoon three-putt on a hole that has figured so prominently in the history of American golf can be forgotten. Strange stepped forth on this acreage where Ouimet and Boros etched their names into the history books and he took his place beside them for posterity. ♀

ONE OF THE GOLF WORLD'S most treasured barometers for course conditioning is called the "Stimpmeter," which measures how fast balls are rolling on putting surfaces. The tool was the brainchild of Edward Stimpson, the 1935 Massachusetts Amateur champion and longtime member of Brae Burn Country Club in Newton. He came up with it in the 1930s, though it took the US Golf Association more than 40 years to adopt it and integrate it into the game.

1988 US Open

YES, VIRGINIA, HE'S REAL

August 7, 1997 • By JIM McCABE

There are times — perhaps not often, but enough to make you wonder — when golf disappoints. Too many golf carts clutter the fairways, and a game that gave us Francis Ouimet is saturated with too many players who fudge scores to push up their handicaps for those ghastly calcuttas and scrambles.

The game is not spoiled, but we are. It is easier to ride than walk. It is easier to take a 4-foot putt than make it. It is easier to buy a teacher's video than hit a bucket of balls.

Titanium drivers, bubble shafts, and ridiculously priced balls that are powered, I guess, by nuclear energy. They're all out there.

Pro players get million-dollar endorsements for pitching golf gloves that don't help a lick, and if you have the time, they'll tell you how greens are too fast, rough too high, fairways too narrow. They'll say all this, of course, as they drive away in their courtesy cars.

It makes you wonder where the game is headed. Until it leads you to a Mike Silverman, who, even as a 14-year-old incoming freshman at Newton North High School, could suddenly remind you of everything that has made golf the great game it is.

He showed up at Brae Burn Country Club in Newton, Massachusetts, one day in the summer of 1997 when street lights were still on. All he wanted was a chance to get on a bag, to caddie in the 97th United States Women's Amateur. He got what he wanted, and more. He got an audience with a few members of the media, a little bit of the spotlight, and a front-row seat in the writing of another chapter to golf's history.

In these days of hefty greens fees and power carts, the caddie is an afterthought. This is sad, because the caddie is so important to golf, so much an irreplaceable part of its history. To many, the greatness of golf forever will be captured in the most famous picture in the sport's history — young Eddie Lowery, golf bag slung over the shoulders, walking beside Francis Ouimet in the 1913 US Open. They shared a spectacular victory, then a lifelong friendship.

Photos of Mike Silverman and Virginia Derby Grimes will never be as famous, but they worked quite an act over at Brae Burn.

Silverman was not scheduled to be on Grimes's bag, but when her regular caddie did not show up, the call went out to the 4-foot-10-inch, 83-pounder. He tackled his duties with vigor and enthusiasm that made you smile. No wonder he moved from novice to C- to B-grade caddie in less than a year.

You drive from an elevated first tee at Brae Burn, right in front of the clubhouse, and it's the most popular spot to watch. So there was a small crowd watching when Grimes split the fairway at 8:33 on a Monday morning. She trudged downhill, her driver in hand. Right behind her came Silverman, almost running to keep up, tugging a bag seemingly bigger than him. If Grimes appeared focused on her task, she was no more so than Silverman.

Take and store all those Nike ads and 320-yard Tiger Woods drives. This was the best promotional view the game could have.

Silverman tended all the pins, raked the traps, wiped off the ball, and always kept up. Did he help with club selection? "No, I pretty much do that," said Grimes, who toured these fabled links in 70-72 to take medalist honors. "But he's great out there. We talk and he keeps me going. And he's great on the greens."

The 18th green at Brae Burn is as tough a test as you'll ever putt. Rule No. 1: Don't be above the pin. Rule No. 2: Don't ever forget Rule No. 1. But Grimes was just above the pin at one point, looking at a sliding downhiller from inside of 10 feet. "He told me to pick out a spot just in front of the hole, then just get it rolling. I said, 'OK, you've got it.' "

Grimes slipped it in for one of the rare birdies at this great finishing hole, a 1-under 72 securing her position as medalist by one shot.

If he was helpful on the greens, perhaps it's because Silverman had an old recipe for success: hard work. "We were walking off the first tee in the second round, 12:33 p.m.," said Grimes, "and he told me he knew where all the pins were, what tiers they were on, and where they were tucked.

"I said, 'You do? How do you know that?' He said he came out earlier in the morning and walked the course. Imagine a 14-year-old kid doing that. I was impressed." ⚲

NEW ENGLAND WOMEN DOMINATED the formative years of the National Amateur Championship, with Massachusetts sisters Margaret and Hariot Curtis being trailblazers for generations to come. Born in Manchester-by-the-Sea, Margaret and Hariot combined to win four US Women's Amateur titles and their match in 1907 remains the only championship contested by sisters (Margaret won). Ten years after Margaret won the last of her three titles, Connecticut-born and Rhode Island-raised Glenna Collett Vare captured the first of her record six US Women's Amateur championships.

en's Amateur

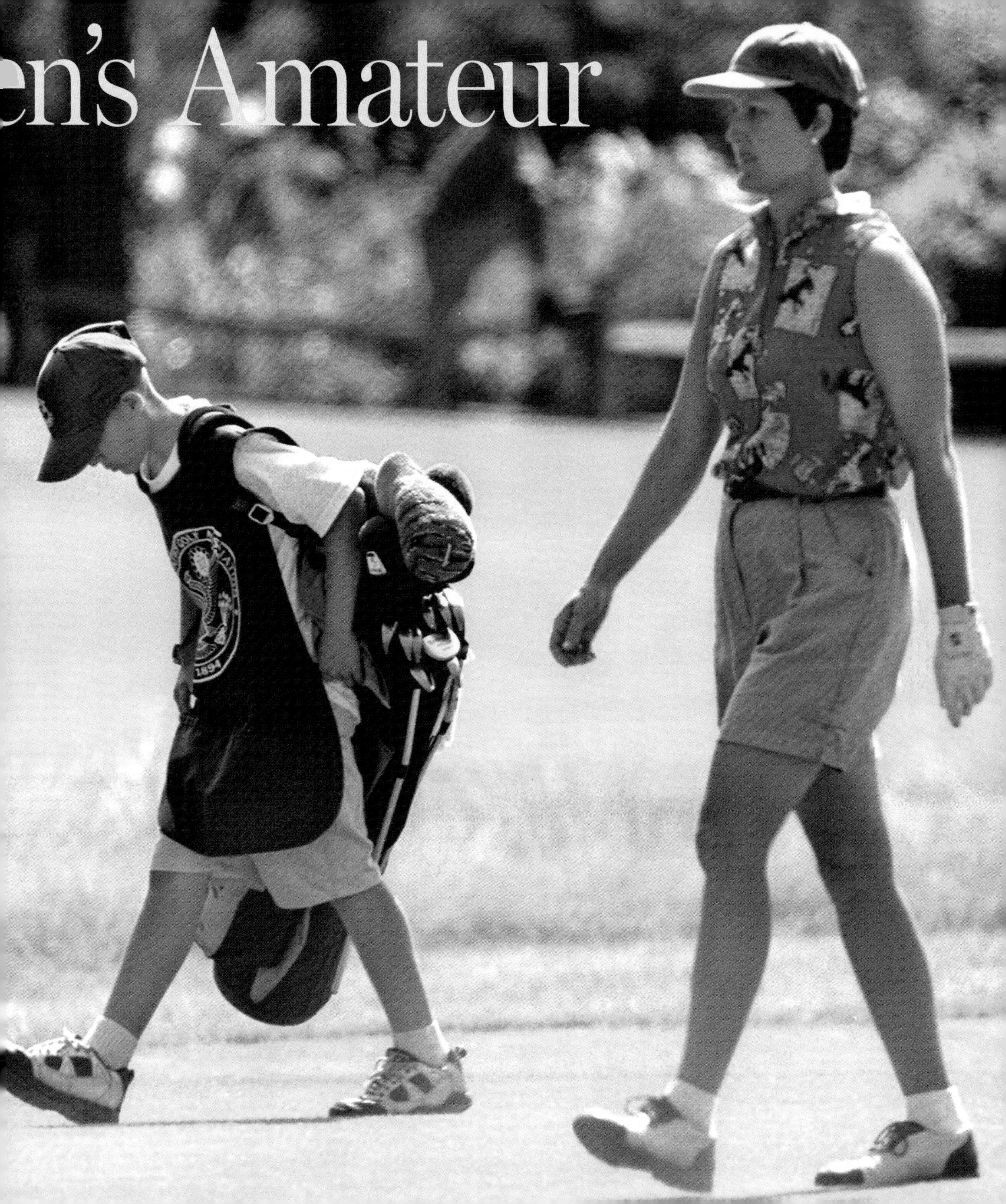

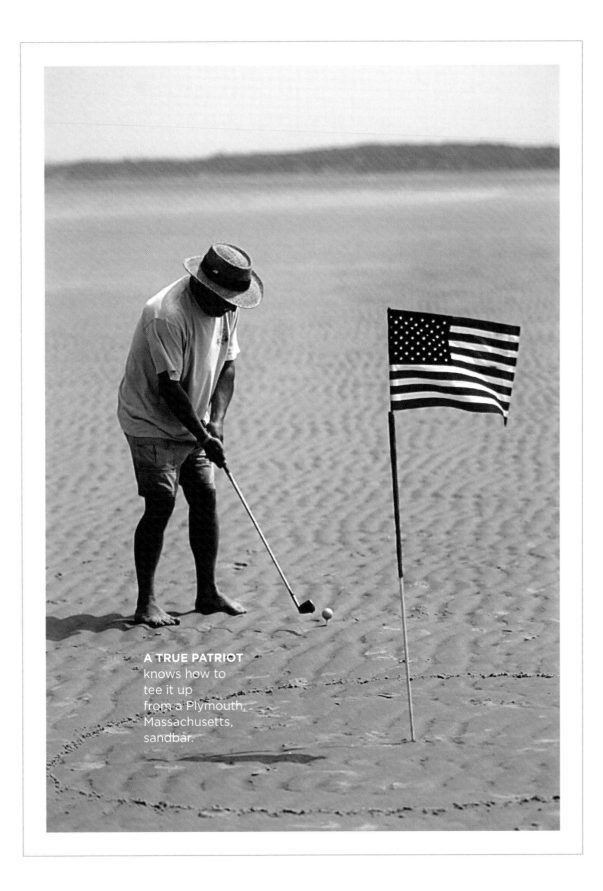

A TRUE PATRIOT knows how to tee it up from a Plymouth, Massachusetts, sandbar.

A WIN AT WANNAMOISETT

August 19, 2001 • By JIM McCABE

Every year around PGA Championship time, we like to reflect on some of the folks who paved the way for today's young millionaires. This includes Tom Creavy, 1931 champion.

"People probably never heard of him because he had such a short career," said another Tom Creavy (the champ's nephew), who lives on Cape Cod. "But he had a good career. And we took a lot of pride in his victory."

There's a third Tom Creavy involved in this story, so it'll get confusing unless we set up the lineage. Here goes:

The elder Tom Creavy is the guy who at 20 years of age stunned the golf world by beating first Gene Sarazen in the semifinals, then Denny Shute in the final of the 1931 PGA Championship. It was played at Wannamoisett Country Club in Rumford, Rhode Island, and mementos of that dramatic victory still adorn the stately clubhouse.

Creavy the 1931 winner (and future head pro at Albany CC) grew up in Westchester, New York, one of seven children in a golf-happy family. His brothers were Joe, who apprenticed under Willie MacFarlane and Tommy Armour and served as head pro at The Sagamore Club at Lake George; Bill, the longtime head pro at Bonnie Briar CC in Scarsdale; and Jack, who didn't turn pro but won the New York State Amateur.

Joe Creavy had one son, also named Tom, who settled in Massachusetts and became a member at the Hyannisport Club. This Tom Creavy named his son Tom also, and the son lived up to his legacy as a semifinalist in the State Amateur and the low amateur in the State Open.

Tom Creavy the great-nephew takes great pride in his family name. "I run into guys frequently who remember my uncles," he said. "They were sort of a legendary family of golfers in the Metropolitan [New York] section."

The 1931 PGA Championship was played in September, and the usual array of stars was on hand. Walter Hagen was past his prime then, ousted in the first round, but Sarazen was at his best. The defending champ was Armour, the classy Scotsman, and Leo Diegel had won in 1928-29. Paul Runyan, Horton Smith, and Shute were all there, as was a young kid from New York. Not much was written about Tom Creavy, but to followers of the very strong Met section, he wasn't a nobody; as a 17-year-old, he had defeated reigning US Open champ Johnny Farrell in the Met Open.

After shooting 148 to finish fourth in qualifying and marching through Jack Collins (5 and 4), Peter O'Hara (2 up), and Cyril Walker (3 and 1), Creavy found himself in the semifinals. Boston papers characterized Creavy as a minor roadblock to a ballyhooed final matchup between Sarazen and Shute. But Creavy dispatched Sarazen, 5 and 3.

"Day after day, with a firm, sound swing and remarkable control around the greens, he continued to cut down [the heralded names]," reported The Boston Globe on September 20, 1931, recounting Creavy's win over Shute.

Creavy had a 4-up cushion through 30 holes, but Shute won the 31st hole with a par and the 33d hole with a birdie. A double bogey at the 34th hole had narrowed Creavy's lead to one hole, and the crowd sensed that a collapse was in the offing.

But no. Creavy prevailed at the 35th hole when Shute made a double bogey, and among the first to congratulate the 20-year-old was the referee, none other than Bobby Jones. "It was one of the finest matches I think that was ever played," Jones told Creavy, who became the second-youngest player to win the PGA Championship. (In 1922, Sarazen was 20 years, 5 months; Creavy was 20 and 7 in 1931.)

The most obscure PGA champion ever? Perhaps, though this wouldn't mean Creavy was an undeserving champion. He did, after all, play five 36-hole matches after going 36 in medal play to get in. Fluky things happen over 18 holes of match play, but rarely over 36. Newspaper accounts of his win over Shute praised Creavy's birdie putts on the 10th and 11th holes, of 30 and 35 feet, as proof that he was a worthy champ.

His upset of Farrell a few years earlier had proven his skill, and nothing Creavy did in the subsequent seasons tarnished his reputation. In 1932, for instance, Creavy stormed into the semifinals of the PGA, only to fall behind by eight holes to Frank Walsh. Undaunted, Creavy made five birdies late to force overtime, but fell on the 38th hole. The next year, Creavy again made it into the semifinals, losing to Jimmy Hines. He'd never play in the PGA Championship again.

"He developed back problems, then got spinal meningitis," said Tom Creavy the nephew. "Then he lost his hearing."

Tom Creavy the 1931 champ settled into a successful career as a teacher and died in 1979.

"Everyone in the family was always proud of my great-uncle's win at Wannamoisett," said the great-nephew. "He was a very well-respected teacher."

And forever he'll be a champion. ⚲

THRILL AT BLUE HILL

August 10, 2006 • By JIM McCABE

After playing 155 holes over five days to beat seven opponents and prevail over a field of 127 at the 38th PGA Championship, Jack Burke Jr. got a check that was worthless.

"Imagine that? The check was hot, no good," said Burke. "I don't know who was responsible for backing up the purse, but the PGA had to make it good."

It was some 50 years ago that the PGA Championship rolled into Blue Hill Country Club in Canton — "Porky's club," said Burke, a nod to legendary head pro Ed "Porky" Oliver. It marked the only time the PGA Championship played out in Massachusetts, and without question it's a happy memory, bounced check and all.

Since he had won the Masters in April, Burke had become just the seventh player to take two majors in a season, but in truth, the Texan was a golfing institution as much for his wit, insight, and straight talk as for his playing record.

"That tournament was the biggest of my career," said Burke. "It gave me a lifetime exemption. That's why winning was important. Hell, they could have had the money."

The 1956 PGA Championship (then a match-play event) had a handful of local subplots: Bill Ezinicki lost in Round 1 to Mike Turnesa; Hap Malia won his first-round match, then was ousted by Jack Fleck; Jim Browning and Johnny Thorne also won opening matches, only to lose their next ones. But it was the presence of the game's giants that made it the show it was.

Sam Snead had won three PGA Championships and was still a force when he rolled to three straight wins to set up a match with Gene Sarazen, then 54. The Squire was no match for the 44-year-old Snead, who cruised, 5 and 4, but it would be as far as he'd go. Ted Kroll ousted Snead in the quarterfinals.

Snead wasn't the first big name to be beaten. Jimmy Demaret was bounced in the second round, as was Doug Ford, the defending champion. Tommy Bolt was beaten in the first round, while Claude Harmon fell in Round 3.

The PGA Championship would use the match-play format one more time, then in 1958 it switched to stroke play, but to the men who experienced it, it's a badge of honor to have maintained the stamina that match play required.

No one can attest to that more than Burke, who in 1955 had been on the losing end of a nine-hour, 40-hole epic match in the quarterfinals of the PGA Championship to Cary Middlecoff.

For a while, it appeared as if 1956 would bring a repeat, because in his semifinal struggle with Ed Furgol, Burke went 37 holes — only, this time he won. He had been 5 down through 14 holes in the morning 18, then 2 down at the break, only to win five straight holes midway through the afternoon portion to regain the momentum.

"That's what I'm most proud of," said Burke. "Coming back from being 5 down to Furgol."

He was also down by two holes in his final match against Kroll when the morning 18 ended and it was time for lunch. "I stayed on the putting green. My caddie [Newton firefighter Italo Amicangioli] got me a milk shake and cookies, but I just stayed there putting. I had putted so badly in the morning."

The diligence paid off. After losing the first hole of the afternoon round to go 3 down, Burke won five of the next seven and went on to win, 3 and 2. It earned him the Wanamaker Trophy and he eventually got paid, too. The lasting respect from his colleagues? Well, Burke had probably secured that years earlier, and he has never lost it, not even after retiring from fulltime competition at the age of 34 to build Champions Golf Club in Houston with Demaret.

"My old man had a philosophy," said Burke, from his office at Champions. "Look, when you get to the top of the tree, you've got to climb down. Now, you can fall down and break a lot of limbs, or you can come down without breaking them."

Burke chose the latter, but he isn't afraid of bruising egos with his blunt talk. He has been around the game for nearly all of his life and cares little for some aspects that shape the contemporary landscape. For example, he's fearful that a player on a practice range somewhere is going to get seriously hurt by a teaching device — what with all the ropes and metal — and he feels pity for what they've done to the club professional's job description.

As for the phenomenon called Tiger Woods, Burke said it isn't a mystery.

"He's the only one who understands how to play the game, how to make shots," said Burke. "The other guys? They're all out there plumb-bobbing the world, worrying about their launch angle and their ball speed. But Woods is like the great pool player: He doesn't see the cue, doesn't see the ball, he just sees the whole game."

Though Burke pretty much left the weekly grind of the PGA Tour the year after his conquest at Blue Hill CC, he remained a fixture at the PGA Championship through 1973. He has had a Hall of Fame life through and through, and if you want to suggest that the highlight was his five days at Blue Hill CC half a century ago, he would not argue with you. ⚲

YOUNG TIGER'S ROAR

August 2, 1992 • By MICHAEL VEGA

Because his game was mechanical, precise, and without any perceptible flaws, there was a mistaken tendency to think that this skinny 16-year-old kid from Cypress, California, was not human. That he was not subject to raw human emotions. That there were no chinks in his suit of armor.

But in the 1992 finals of the 45th US Junior Amateur Championship at Wollaston Golf Club in Milton, Massachusetts, Tiger Woods proved that he was human, indeed, when he rallied from a sluggish start and a two-hole deficit with five holes remaining to become the first player ever to repeat as champion.

And when he tapped in a 3-foot bogey putt on the 18th to defeat Mark Wilson, 1 up, Woods turned and hugged his caddie/sports psychologist, Jay Brunza, then collapsed into the waiting arms of his father, Earl, buried his head, and softly wept.

"Just like Faldo," Tiger said, referring to Nick Faldo's emotional victory in the British Open. "You can't believe how much tension there was out there. Now it's finally over. It just all came out. ... It feels pretty damn sweet to repeat."

What made it sweeter was that Woods waged an epic battle in his championship match against Wilson, a 17-year-old from Menomonee Falls, Wisconsin, to do it.

After reaching the finals by defeating Todd Lynch, 16, of Winston-Salem, North Carolina, 5 and 4, Wilson rattled Tiger's cage by going 2 up after the first two holes when Woods bogeyed both holes. It was the first time all week he had trailed.

"I knew he'd come back," Wilson

said. "I knew about his reputation and I knew about his caddie."

When it appeared his deficit was in danger of growing to three holes after he drove his tee shot into the right rough on No. 3, a 205-yard par 3, Woods saved par with an 8-foot putt to halt his skid.

"That got my juices flowing again," he said.

Woods battled back to finish even at the turn, but when Wilson birdied 11 with a 10-foot putt, and Woods then bogeyed the par-3 12th, he trailed by 2 with six holes to go.

Wilson began to unravel on the 14th when he hit a cluster of trees on his second shot and took a bogey on the par-5 hole. After he hooked his tee shot on 15, Woods rallied by punching his second shot out of the rough and onto the green ("It was a Scottish shot") to halve the hole by saving par.

Woods then came up with his best shot of the day, finally nailing a green when he spun in a wedge shot on 16.

"I thought that one had gone over, too," Woods said, referring to a miscue he had on that same hole in his 3-and-2 semifinal victory against Jonathan Bartlett of Ocala, Florida. "But when I didn't see anyone bail out, I knew it was good."

The shot landed on the green and drew back within 3 feet of the pin for a birdie putt that enabled Woods to even up the match with two holes remaining.

After the players halved the par-3 17th, Woods went left with his tee shot on No. 18, while Wilson found the short rough on the right of the fairway. After Wilson hit his second shot into the left greenside bunker, Woods reciprocated by burying his shot into the right greenside trap. Wilson, however, made a critical mistake when his shot landed on the fringe just beyond the trap.

"When I got into the bunker, all I had were positive thoughts," Wilson said. "I was thinking of getting it within 5 feet, but I decelerated the club and didn't hit it the way I wanted to."

Woods blasted his shot onto the green, 15 feet away from the pin, and putted to within easy bogey distance from 3 feet out. ⚐

Editor's note: In 1993, Woods became the first golfer in history to win three consecutive US Junior Amateur titles.

ANOTHER NOTCH IN NEWPORT

August 28, 1995 • By JOE CONCANNON

The name of Tiger Woods moved higher up in the record books of golf when he won his second straight US Amateur, 2 up, against the dogged Buddy Marucci at Newport Country Club, where the first national championship was contested a century before. At just 19, Woods racked up his fifth United States Golf Association national title.

It was appropriate; Newport CC was one of the five founding members of the USGA and the trophy is named after the first president of the organization, Theodore Havemayer, who was a member of the club. To put Woods's feat into perspective is to point out that just two players won more than five USGA titles in their career: Bobby Jones with nine and Jack Nicklaus with eight.

Woods won six matches and never trailed until Marucci won the seventh hole in the scheduled 36-hole final.

The end came on the 18th green when Marucci missed a birdie putt from 20 feet after Woods hit an 8-iron into the green that backed up to within 1 foot of the cup to the roars of a gallery that had dwindled after a brief downpour with six holes to go. After he missed the putt, Marucci conceded the hole and Woods had an emotional and tearful embrace with his father, Earl, on the green.

Woods's 1994 win at the TPC at Sawgrass in Ponte Vedra, Florida, saw him come back from a six-hole deficit before beating long-time friend Trip Kuehne, 2 up. "They're all different because they were done differently," said Woods. "I had a few things going for me this year. I thought it was easier because I was playing better. It was simple. I knew what I had to do. I had to be very patient."

Marucci was actually 3 up after 12 holes in the morning but lost the 13th and 14th, and they exchanged the 15th (Marucci) and 17th (Woods) to give the Pennsylvanian a 1-up lead at the lunch break. He then won the first hole in the afternoon to go 2 up again. Woods won the third, and the sixth when he knocked it up tight. They turned all square, then Woods won the 12th when he holed a 20-foot putt and the 15th with a birdie. The last hope for Marucci, who had missed a makeable birdie putt on the 16th, was on the 17th when Woods made a bogey 5 set up by two shots out of rough.

The shot on the 18th was one that wins national championships, landing 18 feet above the hole and backing up to 1 foot.

"I do have to say that playing the British Open at St. Andrews and the Scottish Open at Carnoustie helped me a lot," said Woods. "It was so hard in the fairways there. You learn to hit shots in Scotland you can't hit here in America." ⚐

Editor's note: In 1996, Tiger Woods became the first golfer in history to win three consecutive US Amateur titles. He turned pro in August of that year; see Page 142 for that chapter of the story.

swinging new englanders

olf is a game of numbers. It is as simple as that — or so I suggested to Richard Haskell, the former executive director of the Massachusetts Golf Association. "You are what you shoot" was my premise.

With far too much dignity to overrule me, Haskell merely smiled. Then he said, "So far as the competition goes, it's about numbers. That's true. But golf is about people."

He is right. Golf is not about who is shooting the best scores and winning the most lavish championships; it is about the people who play this confounding, yet addicting, game — people whose skill level may not reach all-world status, but whose passion runs so deep that they have made the pastime an integral part of their lives and our sporting landscape.

We who love golf are easily swept up in the game and emotions of those who chase around this little white ball. We feel the pain when someone misses a 3-foot putt and marvel at a player's extraordinary power. We care little for wind, rain, and cold, but totally appreciate how such weather would hardly deter a player from keeping a tee time. We play it as it lies and identify with those who do likewise.

New Englanders have long had a love affair with golf and on the ensuing pages you'll read about intriguing people — New England people — who have treated the game with the utmost respect and who, in return, have felt blessed to be part of it.

Each of them no doubt experienced unfortunate bad bounces and birdie putts that should have gone in, only to catch a piece of the lip and spin out. Each of them, I'm convinced, accepted that golf, like life, has never advertised itself as fair.

Some of these people — such as Francis Ouimet and Leo J. Martin — passed away long ago, yet left legacies that have enriched the game forever. Others I feel fortunate to have spent time with before they died, for they shared pieces of their lives and afforded me a glimpse into the magic that is golf.

Dick Stimets was one such golfer, arguably the grandest gentleman I ever met, and another was Jeff Julian, whose love of the game I only wish could have been bottled for future generations. Instead of being bitter about the cancer that had invaded his body, Stimets was concerned about how his swing wasn't quite what he wanted. And Julian? Though Lou Gehrig's Disease had depleted his muscles, it seemed the furthest thing from his mind. Even when he striped an approach shot during a practice round, he flashed a grin that dispatched more warmth than the sun. He was unable to speak, but his smile told the rich story you get from people who make up the fabric of golf in New England.

—J.M.

The
champ
wore
dreadlocks

September 19, 2005 • By JIM McCABE

Plentiful are the stories of golfers who come out of nowhere, and this is another one. More accurately, it is the story of a golfer who came out of the woods.

The tale involves Martha's Vineyard golfer Tony Jackson and his first attempt at statewide competition, though it's hard to imagine that anything he ever does in golf will be as memorable. After all, how many golfers spend the night sleeping on the course not at it — and in a bunker, no less? And how many show up with a wedge game you'd pay to have? And how many walk to the first tee looking like ... well, let Cobb Carlson tell you.

"When I saw him coming over, I figured he was the caddie for someone in my group," Carlson recalled. "He had on shorts that had mud on them and he wore sneakers. And the dreadlocks? Well, the looks he was getting were hilarious."

Carlson, an avid golfer who plays out of George Wright Golf Club in Hyde Park, Massachusetts, is no stranger to MGA events, in this case a Mid-Am qualifier at Captains Golf Club in Brewster. But he admits to being caught off guard when Jackson introduced himself as his playing competitor and pulled out his driver. And yes, Jackson was aware of the looks he was getting.

"That was my plan of attack," he said, laughing. "Not too many golfers wear dreadlocks."

Then again, more might adopt the carefree hairdo if they spent their nights on the course.

Jackson said he and his brother, Wayne, only got to sleep in the bunker by the 18th hole until early morning. "The sprinklers came on, and we had to push back into the woods," he explained. The brothers had taken the ferry over to Woods Hole the day before, only to discover that Tony's bank had deposited money into the wrong account, so he was unable to use a credit card for the rental car. They might have headed back on the ferry then, but Tony Jackson always had wanted to play in a tournament like this, and Jim Hackenberg, the golf professional at Edgartown Golf Club, had encouraged him to make the leap. So the brothers decided to take a cab from Woods Hole to Brewster.

It was about a $100 fare, which virtually exhausted their finances. With no place to stay, the brothers shrugged and settled into the bunker. They are native islanders who repair pilings and docks for a living, a chore that requires them to wade into the ocean even during bone-chilling winter months. This night beneath the stars didn't seem much of a hardship, especially if playing in a tournament was the reward.

"I've always wanted to try, but I never knew how to go about it," said Jackson, who played on the Martha's Vineyard High School team but mostly honed his game against fellow club members. OK, so he wasn't wearing the pleated pants and the FootJoy Classics. More important, Jackson had a passion that cannot be taught.

"My brother and I used to watch golf before we played, and we loved it. When we were 11, we used to sneak on to Edgartown GC and we'd play the same three holes over and over. Finally,

Mark Hess [the club general manager] came out and said we didn't have to sneak on. We got a membership for after 4:30 [p.m.]."

Edgartown GC is a gem of a course, relatively short, but with well-manicured greens that run 12 on the stimp, though, truth be told, you are hard pressed to hit them in regulation they are so small.

"It was only a few holes into our round when I realized what a great wedge game he had," said Carlson. "I asked him where he got it and he laughed. He told me that nearly every hole for him at Edgartown was driver, wedge, so he got a lot of work at it, because you miss greens there and have crazy lies."

Had the story ended there, it would have been a good one. But what made it even better is the way in which Jackson went about his golf. "He shot lights out," said Carlson, whose round of 77 earned him a spot in the MGA Mid-Amateur Championship, but a whopping seven shots behind his playing competitor and medalist. Jackson, in his first-ever MGA try, shot 70, three better than his nearest competitor.

Over at Edgartown GC, the news was greeted warmly.

"Imagine that," said Hess. "A guy comes out of the woods and wins the golf tournament. How's that for a story?"

It's a terrific story. It has the kid who is self-taught and just wants to play, the club management that embraces such a passion, the club pro who offers encouragement, the competitor who keeps an open mind and whose respect for the game is validated.

And, yes, it is a story complete with dread locks, though we must ask: What's that all about?

"I like them. No particular reason why," said Jackson, laughing. "But they're warm in the winter, I'll tell you that."

IF YOU WANT to play the game at Widow's Walk Golf Course in Scituate, Massachusetts, you can't be afraid to ruffle a few feathers.

The legend of Bobby

May 8, 2003 • By JIM McCABE

Quietly and with little fanfare, a flavorful slice of Massachusetts golf slipped away with the 2003 death of Bobby Knowles at his home in Aiken, South Carolina. He was 88, and to say he was a character of legendary proportions would be an understatement because few people lived life the way Knowles did.

"He was," said longtime golfing companion Charlie Mulcahy, a former vice-president of the Boston Bruins, "an impressive guy who liked life and liked to be around people. And he loved to play golf."

Knowles was a force on the state and national golf scene in the 1940s and '50s, an era when premier players were hardly in a rush to head out to the PGA Tour. They found the challenges and glory abundant enough at the amateur level, and the names that dotted the landscape had talents and skills that commanded respect. Charlie Coe, Dick Chapman, Bill Campbell, Frank Stranahan, Harold Paddock, James McHale, Willie Turnesa, and Sam Urzetta. Giants each, and all of them Knowles's teammates in the 1951 Walker Cup Matches at Royal Birkdale in England.

That was certainly an achievement for which Knowles took great pride, but it was hardly the only highlight on his impressive resume. Not when you consider that he won the Massachusetts Amateur in 1949, the New England Amateur in 1950, and the French Amateur in 1951. He also had terrific runs in the US Amateur and in both 1951 and '52 he earned invitations to the Masters.

But all of that speaks to Knowles's talent and hardly scratches the surface of what truly set him apart from so many of his competitors: his Gatsby-like persona. Knowles was a wealthy man, born in Prides Crossings into a family with a rich New England bloodline. His great-grandfather was Henry Wadsworth Longfellow, his grandfather was J.G. Thorp, runner-up to H.J. Whigham in the second US Amateur in 1896. He was never bashful about his lot, and while some may have been jealous of him, Knowles hardly rubbed folks the wrong way.

"He had good means, but he enjoyed every minute of his life," said Bill Safrin, the longtime head professional at the Myopia Hunt Club in South Hamilton, where Knowles was a fixture for many years.

"Spring golf at Myopia," said Knowles's longtime golfing companion and fellow Myopia member Jim Wyckoff, "didn't begin until Bobby arrived from [spending his winters in] South Carolina. He'd organize the tournaments."

"He was very affable, very confident, very social," said Dick Haskell, the longtime executive director of the Massachusetts Golf Association. "He would tell stories and you'd listen for hours."

When the legend of Knowles is discussed, it is often said that the man never had to work, therefore he didn't. "But that's not true. He did work," said Mulcahy. "He was an auto salesman at one time and he had other jobs, but I think Bobby was devoted to his wife [Barbara Rutherfurd Knowles] and family [daughters Lucy and Alice]. He was very close to his family, he had a very large group of friends, and along the way he had a lot of fun playing golf."

On the local scene, Knowles came along at a time when the stars were career amateurs and players of great skill, men such as Ted Bishop, Johnny Chew, Chapman, and the Martin twins, Leo and Eddie. There was a stint in the Army during World War II, but with the hostilities over, the State Amateur returned to order: Bishop won in 1946, Chew followed, and Eddie Martin in 1948 did what his brother had done in 1941. That set the stage for Knowles in 1949, and when he prevailed at The Country Club in Brookline, he became one of five State Amateur champs who won the event at their home course.

He was very much at ease in social settings, "a friend of everyone's," said Mulcahy, and he was happy to help get things organized, particularly golf tournaments. One that he helped run at Myopia for years featured actor Jack Lemmon, a friend of Knowles's, "and there was very much a sort of nobility to him," said Safrin.

Safrin tells the story of a pro-senior tournament at Essex County Club in Manchester in which Knowles wanted to be included. Since Safrin was already committed to play with another Myopia member, Knowles paired with one of Safrin's young assistants, Tom O'Brien. After the round, Safrin asked O'Brien how they had done, and the young man shrugged.

"I really don't know," said O'Brien. "Mr. Knowles took the scorecard at the very start and said, 'Don't worry. We're going to do OK.'" Safrin laughed at the retelling, because that story, like most of those that involved Knowles, brought back pleasant memories of a man who knew he had a good life and was determined to enjoy it to the fullest with as many friends as possible. For sure, he was OK as long as golf was part of it all. 🏌

MYOPIA ALWAYS attracts a good-looking gallery (above), but Bobby Knowles's biggest fans were his wife and mom (left).

HOT TIPS, COLD PLAY

New England weather has always been an hour-to-hour matter. A course may be fine on a Friday afternoon, but on Saturday, it's another story.

If you want to play in the winter, dress accordingly. Wear a hat, since most of a body's heat loss is through the head. Layers of clothing (knit sweaters) are better than heavy coats. On that note, a thinner golfer has an advantage — the extra layers of clothing will not affect his swing as much as they will a husky golfer.

Another trick to keep your feet warm is to wear plastic bags between two pairs of socks. Winter golf gloves, on both hands, are a must.

F-F-FORE!

Winter golf in the Northeast

December 13, 1996 • By PAUL HARBER

For some golfers — hardy New Englanders — winter golf does not mean flying to Florida. It means braving the bitter cold and trudging along icy fairways.

"It really isn't that cold," they'll declare, their foggy breath betraying their eternal optimism.

While these birds do not fly south, they are acutely aware of the weather. They can tell you precisely where the New England snow line is. They know what courses are open and how many greens are open at those courses.

Every weekend, caravans from Maine, New Hampshire, and Western Massachusetts head out in the morning darkness to bare-ground destinations in hopes of playing a game that resembles golf.

But it isn't golf. It is something else. Ever hit a high shot into a frozen green? When you find your ball — that is, if you find your ball — it will be 20-30 yards beyond the green. It is like hitting a shot in a parking lot. You watch your well-struck iron bounce like a Superball off the concrete-like green and disappear into the vegetation.

"You have to hit a run-up shot," said Jim Gabriel, a winter golf veteran. "It can be tricky because if it gets a little warm and the fairways begin to soften, then your approach shot sometimes buries in the soft turf. Yes, it can be frustrating."

Winter golfers are a hardy breed whose compulsion for the game far exceeds their tolerance for freezing temperatures. Winter golfers don't complain about the weather, they compete with it.

How do you stick a tee into the frozen earth? Some golfers have carried ice picks in their golf bags to make a hole for the tee. Others use upside-down plastic tops of soda pop bottles.

And then there are those savants who purchase winter tees that do not need to be stuck into the earth.

Trying to play golf during a typical New England winter is a challenge, but one whose tradition goes back as far as 1907. At the original Wollaston Golf Club in East Milton, Massachusetts, 25 members turned out that winter to play in what has come to be a popular event, the annual New Year's Day tournament — weather permitting.

Others drive to Cape Cod, where bare ground can often be found even when Boston is blanketed in snow.

The peak months for winter golf are January and February. "I attribute it to three reasons," said Mickey Herron, a veteran Cape Cod golf professional. "First, a lot of golfers get new equipment over the holiday and they are dying to try them out. Second, the PGA Tour … has begun on television, and watching the pros makes you want to get out there yourself. Third, it's basically cabin fever. You can't stand sitting around at home anymore.

"It doesn't matter if the weather turns ugly," added Herron. "If they say the long-range forecast is pretty good, no matter what the weather is, golfers show up."

What does Herron consider a good weekend forecast? "Oh, temperatures in the 40s and a little sun." ⚐

CLOCKWISE FROM TOP LEFT
Golfers drive through snow and cold in East Montpelier, Vermont, and in Massachusetts at Crystal Springs Golf Course in Haverhill, Franklin Park Golf Course in Boston, and Sandbaggers practice range in Pembroke.

WINTERIZING the Leo J. Martin Memorial Golf Course in Weston, Massachusetts.

Twin talents for the ages

October 5, 2000 • By JIM McCABE

The woman's heart had been broken by the sharpest of all pains — the death of a child she had brought into the world — and now she was being asked to relinquish an item in her home that memorialized him.

The man wanted back the trophy and Catherine Martin couldn't stand the thought of letting it go. "It's Leo's," she said through tears, but it wasn't. It belonged to the Massachusetts Golf Association, and as the men quietly grasped the trophy and headed to the door, the woman cried softly, turning toward her son Edward for comfort. "Don't worry," said Edward, for years inseparable from his brother Leo. "I'll bring it back."

This is a story about a simpler time when the world was smaller and people's dreams less extravagant. It is a story of twin brothers who shared a passion for golf, a desire to compete, and a love of each other. It begins on Main Street in Watertown, Massachusetts, where Leo and Eddie Martin would slam golf ball after golf ball up Partridge Street and send their trusty dog Buster to retrieve them, and it ends in the icy waters of the North Atlantic where one brother lost his life and the other lost much of his spirit.

"They were wonderful, wonderful boys," said Kathleen Martin, comforted by memories of brothers who coddled her. Her scrapbooks remember the golfing accomplishments of Leo and Eddie Martin, with page after page detailing their prowess on courses throughout the country, from their domination of local four-balls to their State Amateur victories to their appearances in the National Amateur.

They learned the game as caddies under the tutelage of Johnny Cowan at Oakley CC in Watertown, but when it came time to play, Leo and Eddie Martin could be found at Sandy Burr in Wayland or at two courses that no longer exist — Waltham CC and Trapelo GC in Weston.

Leo made the first splash, winning the 1932 state caddies championship by nine shots after registering a 146 at Commonwealth CC. Two years later, the teenage brothers began what would be a long-running hit act by winning an MGA Four-Ball event at Oakley CC. They were high school seniors and skipped a day of school to compete.

When the Martins followed that Oakley win with a four-ball triumph at Woodland GC in Newton, there was little doubt they were for real. Now, it was left up to reporters to tell them apart.

The consensus was that Leo (6 feet, 190 pounds) was the more talented player, Eddie (6 feet, 205 pounds) a more ferocious competitor. If that's true, it explains why they were so successful as a four-ball team, though off the course they were quite a pair, too, particularly when it came to pranks. Because they looked so much alike, a favorite trick was for Eddie to walk onto the tee and introduce himself as Leo (or vice versa). This routine, however, became harder as their reputations spread, and when the Martin boys advanced to the championship of arguably the area's most important amateur event back then — The Country Club Cup — Fred Corcoran of the MGA instructed that Leo wear a blue sweater while Eddie wore brown.

The man in the blue sweater won, 3 and 1, just as he did the majority of times the brothers met head-to-head. It made reporters curious, for there didn't seem to be much difference between the two. But Eddie was quick to explain: "Sure, we have the same shots, the same distance, the same putting stroke. Everything's the same, I guess. But Leo has something extra inside. It's a gifted ability of concentration, the trick of doing the right thing at the right time."

It was a trick he pulled off a good many times, because from the late 1930s into the early 1940s, Leo and Eddie Martin were arguably the most formidable four-ball team in tournaments that featured marquee names, and their victory in 1937 at perhaps the best four-ball event in the country, The Jaques Cup at TCC in Brookline, solidified their lofty standing.

Mind you, in these days good players did not aspire to be professionals because there wasn't any money in it. Competing against the best amateurs — Francis Ouimet, Fred Wright, Jesse Sweetser, Willie Turnesa, Dick Chapman, Bobby Knowles, Ted Bishop — was the ultimate challenge. So when the 22-year-old twins whipped a team that featured 1936 US Amateur Champion John Fischer in that 1937 Jaques Cup, it was big news.

But it was also a preview of things to come because the Martins kept piling up the victories, qualifying for US Amateurs, and polishing their talents. It ushered Leo Martin into what was a major sports happening in the local area: the 1940 State Amateur championship, where he faced Bishop, a giant in golf circles.

When Bishop dominated, the defeat stung. But at Manchester CC in Vermont weeks later, Leo Martin trounced Tommy Leonard, 6 and 4, for the New England Amateur title. And though Leo again lost to his nemesis, Bishop, in the finals of The Country Club Cup in early 1941, he prevailed in the State Amateur at Longmeadow CC, and a few weeks later the Martin boys won the coveted Winchester Four-Ball.

It took a world war to separate the twins, who enlisted in the winter of 1942 when they were 26 years old. Most of the local four-ball events went

on that year, though the State Amateur was canceled by the MGA, meaning Leo — the 1941 winner — would be "Champion for Duration."

On February 28, 1943, the SS Henry Wynkoop set sail from New York in a convoy, loaded with 8,300 tons of

OAKLEY COUNTRY CLUB

cargo. Seaman First Class Leo J. Martin was aboard for the trip to Belfast, though he never made it. At 3:30 a.m. on March 11, the Wynkoop struck a submerged object in the North Atlantic. A general alarm sounded and members of the crew mistook it for a call to abandon ship. Sadly, no maneuver was necessary, because the vessel was fine. But 33 men had gone into life rafts, and Leo was one of three who never made it back.

Weston's Riverside Golf Links was renamed the Leo J. Martin Memorial Golf Course on October 12, 1945. Catherine Martin attended the dedication.

As for Eddie, he finished his Army stint, returned home and settled in at Winchester CC. Did he get over his brother's death? It probably wasn't possible, but friends submit that golf was a medicine that helped heal the wounds.

When in the summer of 1946 Eddie Martin stood in his mother's house to watch the MGA officials take back the State Amateur hardware that had sat on a family piano since 1941, he made it his duty to win it back.

It took him a few years, but in 1948 Eddie Martin beat Clarence Early at Worcester CC to win the State Amateur. Three years later, he pulled off a rare feat, winning both the State Amateur and the New England Amateur. He qualified for another six US Amateurs and a few US Opens before his death in 1990 at the age of 75, and he got some revenge on Bishop with a victory in The Country Club Cup. No doubt he felt Leo's smile.

And no doubt Eddie Martin knew just where to put the trophy he got for winning the 1948 State Amateur.

"On the piano beside Leo's picture," he said. ♀

leo & ed martin

Hello mudder

March 17, 2002 • By JIM McCABE

There were two days of howling wind, and as each brutal gust swept in stronger than the one before, there was a sentiment among competitors at the 1993 State Mid-Amateur that conditions were borderline unplayable.

So Dick Stimets had a simple game plan.

"I figured when the weather got bad, it was a tremendous opportunity," said Stimets. "I would see people with their chins down and I said to myself, 'Oh, baby, I think I can handle this.' "

Stimets chose not to complain, but to meet the challenge head-on. And all these years later, his effort is part of Massachusetts Golf Association folklore, rounds of 76-70-146 giving him a seven-shot victory at the age of 61. With the wind blowing as much as 60 miles per hour at Willowbend and New Seabury, players struggled to break 80. Stimets's 70 was the only subpar effort of the tournament, and in beating dozens of players half his age, he earned a nod of respect. A great mudder, they will say.

It's the ultimate compliment to a great competitor, and when the memory is brought up, Stimets smiles, then works hard to keep it there. The battle with prostate cancer has been going on for the better part of a decade now, and much like those rounds of golf at Willowbend and New Seabury, he embraces each day as a challenge and says to himself, "Oh, baby, I think I can handle this.

"I try to make every day as full as I can," he said. "When you put the chin down, you bring people down — and I don't want to do that."

So the conversation turns to the game that has been so central to his life, and it takes just a short time to understand how priceless a commodity Stimets is. He has connections to the game that are storybook material, from a caddie's view of Donald Ross, Henry Cotton, and Gene Sarazen, to his prime when he finished third in the Texas Amateur, ahead of youngsters named Ben Crenshaw and John Mahaffey. There was a friendship with Francis Ouimet — first as the great man's caddie, then as a golfing partner — and the treasured times he was in the company of Bill Danforth, a giant of a man who is a story unto himself. There have been countless trips to Bermuda and Scotland with his beloved wife, Ginger, and one of the proudest days of his life was when he got accepted as a member of the Royal & Ancient.

All of it very special, said Stimets.

And all of it because of golf, a game that entered his life in those early teenage years when his father signed him up for a summer caddie camp at The Oyster Harbors Club. He stayed seven seasons. "It was such a marvelous experience, caddie camp," said Stimets. "I learned so many things. I saw the good things in people, and I saw the bad things in people."

It was in 1947 — the year before his death — that Ross visited Oyster Harbors to view the devastation that had struck his layout just a few years earlier. "The hurricane of '44 had wiped out all the trees; everything was flat," said Stimets. "When Ross saw the sixth [hole], he nearly cried. He said it was one of the finest holes he had ever built."

In Ouimet, Stimets saw someone "who was a cut above," a very special man who was still consistently breaking 80 in his early 70s. "I never saw a person who hit the ball so straight so often," said Stimets. He once asked Ouimet if any facet of the game gave him trouble, and the question elicited a pause. "He said he never got the 'sticks,' the Scottish word for 'yips,' " said Stimets. "But finally he said he always had trouble 'working the ball.' That was it. He couldn't work the ball because he hit it so straight."

Ouimet would always offer encouragement and advice, and Stimets took the words to heart. "I tried to model myself after him," said Stimets, and most would say he succeeded. Like Ouimet, Stimets has been the quintessential gentleman golfer, a successful businessman, devoted husband and father, and dedicated volunteer to a number of charitable causes. The club championships number 34 — from Oyster Harbors to New Jersey to Houston to Ohio — and there is a long list of other triumphs in various amateur events.

But more than the competition,

golf has enriched Stimets's life to a point far beyond his wildest dreams. "It's not that all my friends are golfers," said Stimets, "because they're not. But the places I have gone and the people we've met, all because of golf: I've been blessed."

He smiles when he is asked about a story involving Sarazen, for whom he caddied in the late 1940s. Things went wrong while playing the fourth hole, a par 5. After hitting his drive, Sarazen, without conferring with his caddie, gazed at a green and decided to go for it. He reached it, too, except it was the 17th and not the fourth.

"He hit it perfectly, too," said Stimets, laughing, "and boy, he climbed all over me."

Years later, a friend of Stimets's met Sarazen in Naples, Florida, and the Squire noticed the Oyster Harbors logo on the man's sweater. "I played an exhibition there once," said Sarazen. "A son-of-a-bitch caddie gave me the wrong green to shoot at."

There is a hearty laugh, and you can't help but notice that Stimets's chin is indeed up. ⚐

Editor's note: Dick Stimets died in 2002 of cancer. This interview, among his last, is a testament to his spirit.

DICK STIMETS (at left, in dark jacket, shaking hands with Francis Ouimet) made his mark at New Seabury (above).

Good-time Charlie

May 2, 1996 •
BY PAUL HARBER

Charlie Volpone sloshes his way down the 18th fairway at Stow Acres South Course in Massachusetts, dragging a tattered pullcart during the first round of the State Four-Ball Championship.

Plop. Volpone's drive has landed in the middle of the soggy fairway. He takes a drop, and it isn't much better a lie. Volpone and partner Joe Keller are doing their best to ignore an irritating cold April rain. They're more focused on making birdies and avoiding bogeys. Nevertheless, this is not the sort of day you would want to play golf unless you have to play.

Thwack. Volpone muscles his second shot down the par-5 fairway toward the green. His aching back aches just a little more on this damp day … Splat. Volpone's third shot comes up short and nestles in the deep, wet rough that fronts the green.

Despite all the discomfort, Volpone is sporting his usual facial expression — an ear-to-ear grin that might make you think he's enjoying himself on this gloomy morning. He is a golf nut. He doesn't play to prepare for the Senior Tour or a championship tournament. He plays the game simply for the love of the game.

And still, he remembers when the game didn't matter to him at all.

Volpone was 10 years old and living in Newburyport, Massachusetts, where his Aunt Rose was a member at Ould Newbury Golf Club. "It was 1947," says Volpone, "and she thought it would be a good experience for myself and my brother Gerald."

The young Volpone did not agree. "On Mondays the caddies were allowed to play golf, but I didn't bother," he says. "I thought it was a boring game, so I went out and played baseball on Mondays instead."

Eventually, though, Volpone gave the game a whirl. "I went out and shot 69 — for nine holes. That was my first time out," he says.

He began as a caddie and a junior player in the 1940s and was a collegiate golfer at Boston College in the '50s. He tried to make it on the PGA Tour in the '60s and spent time as a club pro at Nashawtuc in the '70s.

After playing in the 1980 PGA Championship, however, Volpone decided on a career change. He quit as a golf professional and entered the insurance business. But he didn't give up the game. Volpone asked the US Golf Association to reinstate his amateur standing.

One part of his game has never changed. He always smiles.

He smiled when he won his first CYO and junior titles at Ponkapoag as well as two State Opens (1971 at Vesper and '72 at Tedesco), a State Amateur ('56 at Belmont) and the Globe Tournament of Club Championships ('57 at Belmont) as well as a host of other tournaments, including the aforementioned '94 State Four-Ball (with Keller at Stow Acres) and the Norfolk County Classic.

Volpone says he would have been happy remaining an amateur his entire career but has some wonderful memories from when he tried to make a living on the PGA Tour. "Why didn't I make it? I think it was money," he says. "In the 1950s you needed backing, about $10,000 at the time, and I didn't have it."

When Volpone looks back at his victories, the championship that is special is his CYO title as a 16-year-old. "I have never felt more satisfaction than winning that tournament at Ponkapoag," says Volpone. He beat Jim Maloney, 4 and 3, in the championship match and was 3-under-par with three holes to play. "Everybody was urging me to play on after the match was decided," says Volpone. "You see, the course record at Ponky was 3-under then, and they thought I could set a new record. I didn't care. Winning the tournament was all I cared about."

Volpone has spent more than a half-century walking New England fairways. He hasn't limited his play to the high-caliber tournaments on the amateur schedule. He plays for fun.

So you can understand why he is always smiling. ♀

When
legends
met

francis ouimet

& bobby jones

July 31, 1997 • By JIM McCABE

He had been a boy wonder himself, just seven years earlier, and Francis Ouimet was living proof of what a fearless young golfer could do.

So as he prepared for his semi-final match in the 1920 US Amateur Championship, Ouimet was respect-ful of his opponent. Though he was a polished player and arguably the country's best amateur at age 27, Ouimet was in no way under-estimating the 18-year-old who stood in his path.

That teen was the incomparable Bobby Jones, and the 1920 match was the first of four head-to-head meetings between these legends.

Better players than Ouimet have graced the golf landscape, but a more gracious person has never walked its fairways. "He was a perfect gentle-man," said Dick Stimets, who caddied for Ouimet and later played golf with him at Oyster Harbors in Osterville, Massachusetts.

The fact that Ouimet had shared the golf stage with men like Jones never figured into their conversation. "I never heard him mention the matches," said Stimets. "But he was so modest, you would never know who he was. He treated everyone, from caddies to opponents, as a friend, and it wasn't his nature to boast."

Ouimet was one of the most beloved players of his generation at a time when the sport was booming in popu-larity. He was a career amateur in an era when that meant you could hold your own against the pros. As a 20-year-old in 1913, Ouimet had become the first amateur to win the US Open. He was quickly followed to the throne by fellow amateurs Jerome Travers (1915) and Chick Evans (1916). Their feats, however, paled in comparison to those of Jones, who won four US Opens between 1923 and 1930.

But to Ouimet, Travers, Evans, Jones, and others of that era, the Open took a back seat to the Amateur. It is often overlooked in the glow of his 1913 triumph, but Ouimet was probably prouder of his US Amateur champion-ships in 1914 and 1931, a 17-year span that ranks as the longest period between victories.

In the 1920 semifinal at Engineers Country Club in Roslyn, New York, Ouimet vs. Jones offered vintage Ouimet, who shot 74 and was 3-up after the morning 18. When he went out in 37 in the afternoon, to Jones's 40, Ouimet was 5-up. He closed out Jones on the 31st hole, but while The Boston Globe sportswriter saw it one way ("Ouimet was far better than the Southern youngster in all depart-ments"), Ouimet felt it came down to one thing: putting. "In 1920 [Jones] was just as great, with the exception of his work on the greens," wrote Ouimet years later. "I must say he was not even a fair putter then."

When they met for the second time, in 1924 at the Merion Cricket Club in Ardmore, Pennsylvania, Ouimet met a player who had a better grasp of the flat stick. The year before, he had won the first of his four US Opens, and by now Jones was the game's prominent player. He had arrived, said Ouimet, thanks to an understanding of match play.

"If he had a weakness at all," wrote Ouimet ... it was simply because he tried to play the man and not the hole. In our semifinal match, he disregarded my play entirely and played against the par of the course."

Oh, how Jones played in that rematch. He was 4-up through nine holes and then won five of the next eight. Ouimet needed a heroic putt on the 18th just to cut Jones's lead to 8-up.

It didn't get any better over the afternoon 18, and the disinterested Boston sportswriter sent the sad news home: "Boston experienced its dismal hours in the semifinals round of the national amateur: Francis Ouimet was badly beaten by Bobby Jones."

It was the worst defeat in Ouimet's storied career, 11 and 10. "What Bobby did to me was criminal," wrote Ouimet. "He was unbeatable and made the winning of holes by me so impossi-ble that I was soundly trounced."

The match was closer, but the result was the same, when they met for the third time, in 1926 at Baltusrol in Springfield, New Jersey. By now, Jones was a national hero of epic proportions, rivaled only by Babe Ruth. He was the two-time defending champion and rode into Baltusrol having won the British and US Opens.

Over the grueling Baltusrol layout, Ouimet was superb. But Jones was better than superb. Though Ouimet matched Jones shot for shot for most of the morning 18, he finished double-bogey, bogey, and was 3-down into lunch.

An outgoing 3-under 34 in the afternoon would have cut into any-body's lead, but Ouimet was not playing just anybody. Jones shot 33. A birdie 2 at the 12th put him 5-up, and he closed out Ouimet on the 32d hole. "To give you some idea of what I was up against," wrote Ouimet, "had I parred out, I would have shot 69, but I was outclassed."

Amazingly, Jones was denied a third straight Amateur title the next day when George Von Elm prevailed, 2 and 1. The upset stung Jones, and he was determined to make amends at the 1927 Amateur at Minikahda in Minneapolis. Unfortunately for Ouimet, it meant a fourth and final match with the kid from Atlanta, who had won his second straight British Open the month before.

Jones, at 25, was a machine. "Positively ruthless," wrote Ouimet. "If you play well, he will go you one better. If the young man were human, he would make a mistake once in a while, but he never makes a mistake. If you can beat that type of man, I should like the recipe."

Jones set the tone on the first hole. Ouimet found the fairway, then the green, and two putts gave him a par. Jones drove into a fairway bunker, made a great shot to the green, and dropped his birdie putt. "From then on it was just a procession," wrote Ouimet, who again lost, 11 and 10.

It would be the last time these legends played head to head. Jones retired from competitive golf after his historic Grand Slam in 1930, though he and Ouimet remained good friends through the years. In 1931, in fact, Jones was one of the first players to congratulate Ouimet when he won his second US Amateur.

In his typical humble fashion, Ouimet was honest about the 1931 proceedings at Beverly Country Club in Chicago. "Removing Bobby ... filled everyone with the idea that he had a chance to win," wrote Ouimet, who took advantage of the chance better than anyone else. He defeated Jack Westland, 6 and 5, in the final.

"When one has made up his mind to accomplish something and it takes 17 years," wrote Ouimet, "the satisfaction is tremendous. I had persevered."

HIGHLIGHTS AND HARDWARE

⌐ He is arguably the most beloved golfer in history and **BOBBY JONES** had two memorable appearances in Massachusetts. In position to win the US Open at Worcester CC, he called a penalty on himself, saying his ball moved in the rough while he stood over it. Praised for his integrity, Jones issued one of his most famous quotes: "You might as well praise me for not breaking into banks." He lost that championship in a playoff, but at Brae Burn CC in West Newton in 1928, Jones put on a dominating show with a 10 and 9 win for the fourth of his five US Amateur titles.

⌐ The first team to represent the US in the Walker Cup — an international team competition for amateur golfers — included three golfers with New England ties: **FRANCIS OUIMET**, New Hampshire native **JESSE GUILFORD**, and **JESS SWEETSER**, who graduated from Phillips Andover and Yale. Ouimet, now a golf legend, is memorialized as the namesake of the trophy (embraced by Bruce Fleisher, at left) given to the winner of the US Senior Open.

America's golf scribe

June 2, 2005 • By JIM McCABE

He had chronicled so many steps by giants of the sport that it seemed as though every significant moment in golf had taken place with Herbert Warren Wind in the audience.

There was, therefore, no shortage of things to ask him. Yet on that warm day a few years ago when he shared his time, the greatest American golf writer had the first question.

"Tell me," said Wind, "is Augusta still beautiful?"

More beautiful than I could have imagined, I told him, and that pleased him greatly. He had made his last visit there perhaps a dozen Aprils earlier, and when he closed his eyes for a brief moment, I knew he was at peace, perhaps recalling so many glorious spring days walking amid the azaleas and Georgia pines. When he opened his eyes, I saw that they sparkled and as Wind leaned in closer, he smiled, then asked, "So what do you want to talk about?"

Golf. I wanted to talk about all the golf he had seen and the many golfers he had known.

"But I'm afraid I don't remember things as well as I once did," said Wind, his voice trailing off. Then, he glanced at a book I had brought, one about Bobby Jones, and he gently picked it up and turned some of the pages. It was as if the photos of Jones had rekindled a spark that had burned inside of him for parts of six decades because Wind nodded his head.

And then he proceeded to talk about the golf he had seen and the golfers he had known.

When he died recently at his home in Bedford, Massachusetts, at the age of 89, Wind left a rich legacy. Fortunate are those who cherish both golf and the written word because few writers treated prose about the game with the care that this Brockton, Massachusetts, native did. Great writing is art that lives forever, so it is that the articles, stories, and books penned by Wind are still available.

He came to love the game as a youngster. Thorny Lea Golf Club was within walking distance in his hometown, and Wind was skilled enough that he played in a British Amateur. But his passion was writing, and despite the objections of his father, who owned a leather company, Herbert Warren Wind tackled his chosen profession with a conviction that resulted in his inimitable style.

"He had such a vibrant mind," Ben Crenshaw told me a few years ago. "I've always considered him the Bernard Darwin counterpart in America."

Funny that Crenshaw should say that, because Wind considered Darwin an icon and meeting him was the turning point in his life. Having graduated from Yale, Wind was a student at Cambridge University in England when he came to know Darwin, and the 22-year-old was swept away.

In the late 1940s, after a stint in the Army, Wind joined the staff at The New Yorker. He was with Sports Illustrated from 1954-1960, but returned to The New Yorker and soon became legendary for his exhaustive essays on sports, most frequently golf, until his retirement in 1990.

His long pieces contained exquisite detail, historical relevance, and insightful commentary. He wrote in a dignified and proper manner that matched his personality: Adorned in tweed suit coat, white shirt and tie, and ever-present hat, Wind would always carry a walking stick, a notebook, and a pencil when he walked the golf courses of his travels, and very little got past him. Glancing through notebooks he once kept, I noticed drawings of golf holes.

Soft-spoken, Wind was the ultimate gentleman who counted Jones among his closest friends. Gene Sarazen, Francis Ouimet, Ben Hogan, Jack Nicklaus, Richard Tufts, and Robert Trent Jones Sr. They, too, were friends.

"The game has changed, hasn't it?" he asked at the end of lunch that day.

I told him it still had wonderful people and marvelous places, but I couldn't lie: It had changed from the days he had cherished.

Wind smiled and said, "I saw so many wonderful things. I was fortunate to be around the game when I was."

No, the game and those of us who love to read about it are the fortunate ones.

LIVING BY THE LEAF RULE

It would be a terrible indictment of our integrity to say we don't adhere to the US Golf Association's fabled "Rules of Golf." It's just that we New Englanders long ago discovered a need for some slight addendums to the manual, even if the USGA has never adopted them.

For instance, we are permitted to play by "winter rules" and provide ourselves relief when we come up against frozen turf, snow, puddles, mud, and other effects related to Mother Nature's colder side. "Winter rules" are roughly limited to coincide with the season (December 22 to March 20), and it's strictly a geographical thing. That means you cannot play "winter rules" in Florida just because it's January 26.

As for the "leaf rule," that, too, is a necessary component of our golf landscape, though with leaf blowers and other modern technologies this New Englandism is needed less and less. In short, the rule allows us a free drop if we are absolutely sure that our ball is buried under one of the thousands of colorful leaves carpeting the ground (at Easton CC in the photo, at left). Again, we must use great discretion; after all, we need to keep our integrity.

The quiet man

July 5, 2001 • By JIM McCABE

Sitting at a table in the back room of a clubhouse on a Falmouth, Massachusetts, golf course that has been his life for more than 25 years, the great man listens to a visitor's suggestion that perhaps a case of bad timing had ushered him through life.

After all, he played on the PGA Tour long before big money and fame entered the picture. And the Senior PGA Tour, that golden parachute for many men just like him, wasn't a profitable endeavor until after his game had left him. Perhaps if he had been born 10 years later ...

The suggestion hangs in the air as Paul Harney takes a drag on another cigarette and slowly shakes his head. His eyes meet yours and at that moment you know that your assumption is wrong; Harney wouldn't trade his life for anyone's.

"No regrets. Not a one," said Harney. "I was so very lucky. I enjoyed playing and when I played well, which I did an awful lot of times, it was so enjoyable."

The stare is long and effective. He means what he says. No regrets whatsoever. Golf was golf, but life was life.

"A father should be with his family," he said.

By all accounts, professional golf moved into the high-speed lane on a Saturday afternoon in June of 1960. Cherry Hills Country Club in Denver, the US Open, and Arnold Palmer drove the par-4 green at the first hole, shot a final-round 65, and thus poured the foundation for a career that has helped shape American sports.

Playing alongside Palmer that unforgettable day was an unassuming Bay State native from the Worcester area. Paul Harney was at 143 after 36 holes, eight shots behind Mike Souchak. Palmer, too, was at 143, paired with Harney for the 36-hole finale. Each of them shot 72 in the morning, but in the afternoon, Palmer posted his incredible round while Harney shot 71 to settle into a tie for 12th. Palmer, of course, rode a meteor that still blazes.

Harney? Well, he proved that day what he already had proven and would prove many more times: While he was quiet enough to be overlooked, he was great enough to be part of the show.

It's one of the memories that sits with him these days as he checks things out at Paul Harney's Golf Club in Falmouth, the executive-style course he has owned since 1964, the one he retired to in 1974 after seven PGA Tour wins. Harney can look back on many huge career moments, but it was a victory in 1956 that opened the most doors.

"The Egyptian Match Play," said Harney.

As in Egypt? The Middle East?

"Fred Corcoran set it up," said Harney, referring to the legendary Boston sports figure who is given credit for the birth of the PGA Tour. "He was involved in international golf events, and he asked for two aspiring young pros to play two tournaments [in the Middle East]."

Bobby Locke was in the field. Harry Bradshaw, too. But here came an unheralded kid named Paul Harney, holding the trophy — not to mention an invitation into the Colonial. It was there that he met Ben Hogan.

"I watched him on the practice tee," said Harney. "He was there until dark. He was my idol. Hell, he was everyone's idol."

It may be his favorite story from a lifetime of rich, rewarding ones: the practice-round saga with Hogan. Harney said he made a par at the first hole then didn't make anything better than bogey in a round so poor that the kid from Worcester felt embarrassed. "I mean, I was absolutely atrocious," he said.

Yet, the next day they played again, and for the second day in a row, Hogan barely said a word to Harney, who again made par at the first hole, then strung together nothing but bogeys and double bogeys. "I don't even know if I was breaking 100, but he wasn't saying a word and that's what was annoying me," Harney said.

Then, at the 18th hole of their second practice round, Harney made another par, his second of the day. "Hogan looked at me and said, 'Son, you're improving.'"

He had won four times on Tour and been a consistent money-winner when, in 1963, Harney decided to step away. There were three children by now, and while his wife, Patty, never voiced a word of discontent, Harney quit the road and took a job at Sunset Oaks Country Club in Sacramento.

"The contract only allowed me to play eight Tour events a year," said Harney. Thrown into that mix was another close call at the US Open, the 1963 edition at The Country Club in Brookline, where his closing bogey left him one shot out of a three-way play-off involving Palmer, Jacky Cupit, and the eventual tournament winner, Julius Boros.

"I'll never forget the day," said Harney. "But I guess it wasn't meant to be."

If that disappointment had a silver lining, it was playing in front of the home crowd. Harney thoroughly enjoyed being back in the area, so in 1965, when he was offered the job as head pro at Pleasant Valley in Sutton, he jumped at the chance.

During his days at Pleasant Valley, Harney's PGA Tour stops were a family affair, about 12-14 events a year, one long ride in the station wagon after another. If there was an annual highlight, it was Augusta National. Harney had made his Masters debut in 1959 and his 12 appearances were a microcosm of his career: never a sensation, but a formidable player. Four times he was top 10, nine times top 20, and only in his final berth, in 1974, did he miss the cut.

By then, he was playing only because of that wild event in 1972 when, at age 42, Harney had won the San Diego Andy Williams Open. A stunner to colleagues, but not to the prideful guy from Worcester.

In 1974 he became the first member of the New England PGA to be named national professional of the year. In 1977, he played in his final two PGA Tour events, then later that summer won his fifth and final Massachusetts Open.

Senior golf just never seemed to fit. He tried, teaming with Jack Burke Jr. in one of the first Legends events at Onion Creek in Austin, but something was missing. He had once played the game at the highest level, going into the heat of competition with guys named Hogan and Palmer, and now... now he was having problems he never had experienced.

"One day I went out and hit it fat, then thin. I had never thought about hitting it fat or thin in 40 years," said Harney, his once jet-black hair a distinguished white. "I just lost interest in playing. I don't care to play."

Today there are numerous grandchildren to spoil and no shortage of great memories.

A smile lights up the room. It belongs to a man who once played golf with a priceless splendor, but never lost sight of his place in life. ♀

IF GOLFERS COULD REWRITE THE RULE BOOK ...

Step aside, PGA Tour commissioner. You gentlemen who run the US Golf Association and the Royal & Ancient also can take the day off. We asked some players: If you could take a turn as CEO of the golf world and rewrite one rule of the game, what would you change?

⚲ "I would change the 10-second rule when the ball is on the lip of a hole," said Robert Allenby, much-decorated PGA Tour winner from Australia. "I don't see how that is any different from any other shot we hit, when we have 35 or 40 seconds. Why is a putt different? It's a stupid rule [penalizing a player for waiting more than 10 seconds to tap in a putt hanging on the lip] and it's cost quite a few guys."

⚲ Brian Gay, another PGA Tour veteran, wants relief when his ball rolls into a divot hole that's been filled with a mixture of sand, seed, and fertilizer. "If there's sand, then it's ground under repair," said Gay. "We should get a drop."

⚲ Chris Smith disagrees. "I don't have a problem with sand in divot holes," he said. "I would change the rule about not being able to knock down spike marks [on greens]." Current Rules of Golf allow players to repair damage made by balls landing on the green, but they cannot pat down those pieces of turf that pop up when metal spikes dig in.

⚲ With a shrug, Peter Lonard figures he's most bothered by players being disqualified for signing incorrect scorecards. "We have walking scorers, official scorers, everyone knows what we shot. It's golf, not an accounting class."

⚲ "We need to change the rule about a lost ball," Jay Haas said. "If you drop the ball you're playing with and it rolls into a hazard, you'd be penalized for a lost ball. It's a silly rule and needs to be taken out. I understand why the rule was there, to stop guys from constantly taking out a ball that gets marked up, but I can't think of the last time when a ball had a cut on it."

⚲ "I would want a unified ball," Billy Mayfair said. "Everyone plays the same ball."

⚲ "No cuts," said Duffy Waldorf. "Never. Everyone gets to play all 72."

⚲ "I'd love to wear shorts," said veteran Joe Durant. "Hey, our legs are not that bad."

⚲ "I'd like a mulligan every nine holes," said Zach Johnson, "... just for me."

Hey, we asked.

PAT BRADLEY
(left) and
Patty Sheehan
celebrate at the
18th hole of the
2005 BJ's Charity
Championship.

WORLD GOLF HALL OF FAME
*members who were born in
New England:*

1913 US Open champion
Francis Ouimet
Brookline, Massachusetts.

Former PGA Tour manager
Fred Corcoran
Cambridge, Massachusetts.

LPGA Tour legend
Pat Bradley
Westford, Massachusetts.

LPGA Tour star
Patty Sheehan
Middlebury, Vermont.

Six-time US Women's
Amateur champ
Glenna Collett Vare
New Haven, Connecticut.

1938 Masters champion
Henry Picard
Plymouth, Massachusetts.

Three-time major winner
Julius Boros
Bridgeport, Connecticut.

Financer behind Pinehurst
No. 2 in North Carolina
Richard Tufts
Medford, Massachusetts.

sally quinlan

Back in the game

September 11, 2003 • By JIM McCABE

Back when she was a bright-eyed Cape Cod child and her special gift and burning passion for the game were unmistakable, Sally Quinlan probably wouldn't have been so moved by a casual round of golf.

But on a summer day in 2002, accompanied by the man who had nurtured her game, Bob Miller, and enjoying the ambiance of Cummaquid during a rare visit to Cape Cod, she remembers being consumed by a single thought.

"I said to myself that day, 'I love this game again,' " Quinlan recalled. "For the first time in years, the thought of going out to play wasn't so horrible. I wanted to play — purely for the fun of it."

Hadn't golf always felt this way? Hadn't this sort of emotion carried her through her dominating amateur career in Massachusetts, through the University of Miami, then onto the LPGA Tour?

Surprisingly, no.

The onetime junior phenom from Dennis, Massachusetts, had long ago separated herself from the game she had played so well. In 1990, just two tournaments into her seventh LPGA Tour season, Quinlan walked away without warning. Having waged a successful battle with alcohol dependency just a few years earlier, she didn't have that same fire to combat the fears that infiltrated her spirit on the course. There had been one LPGA Tour win, a handful of top-10 finishes, and several financially rewarding seasons, but Quinlan saw a bigger picture and it didn't include sweating out 5-foot putts.

The game had not failed her. She never felt that way. But she had failed to keep caring about the game.

Instead, her passion was directed toward social causes and a series of jobs that gave her a sense of fulfillment she had never achieved through golf. For more than 12 years, Quinlan was far removed from golf, including time employed as the director of development for Siloam Ministries, an interfaith organization in Philadelphia that offers a spirituality-based wellness program to people with AIDS.

People who knew her as the teenager who had played golf almost on a daily basis were probably surprised that she had walked away from it all. Those who had watched the kid achieve success at almost every step — from state junior champion in 1978 to state amateur champ in 1979 to New England amateur champ in 1982 — were likely surprised to hear that from 1990 to 2002, she had played no more than once a year. And then, just as quickly as she left the sport, she surprised everyone by returning to it.

That casual round with Miller at Cummaquid rekindled flames that eventually sent Quinlan on a cross-country journey to California, where she took a part-time job as assistant to the executive director of the Ventura County Junior Golf Association and a teaching job at nearby Saticoy Golf Club.

You don't get named to those contrived lists of America's top golf instructors by teaching kids at unheralded public facilities like Saticoy, but Quinlan is every bit as passionate about the game as in those days when she lived at Dennis Pines. She said she plays a set of Ping irons that are more than 15 years old, that she usually shoots 75-78, and that she doesn't hit it on the clubface consistently, but when she does, "I tell myself, 'That's beautiful.'

"It's been a wild ride," she said. "I'm back playing the game purely for the joy of playing the course." ⚐

WHICH NEW ENGLANDER had the most memorable season ever? It would be hard to argue against the late, great Ted Bishop. In 1946 he won the Massachusetts Amateur on July 13, the New England Amateur on August 4, then the US Amateur on September 14.

SURVEYING
the Boston
skyline from the
18th at Granite
Links Golf Club

Rinks and links

October 10, 2002 • By JIM McCABE

It is a warm and gentle handshake, yet when Bill Ezinicki embraces you, there is no mistaking the strength with which he takes hold. This is the contrast that has always shaped his life, because few athletes in our time have offered the diversity of excellence that Ezinicki has.

Gentleman golfer, ferocious hockey player.

Could it be? Could this man they called "Wild Bill" for his penchant for throwing bone-crunching body checks, a man who had an insurance policy that paid him for each stitch he received and whose violent encounters with Maurice "Rocket" Richard and Ted Lindsay are legendary, be the same graceful, quiet golfer who treats the game and all its players with a heralded respect?

Indeed, they are one and the same.

"I could never get over that. His reputation doesn't go with how he was on the golf course," said Paul Harney, arguably the greatest of all Massachusetts golfers. "He was a real gentleman."

Still is, too. As beloved a figure as there is on the local golf landscape, Ezinicki can be found these days at The International in Bolton, Massachusetts, retired after nearly 30 years as head professional, but very much at the soul of this marvelous facility. Ezinicki will answer requests for lessons and for guidance, and while the playing days have ebbed, he is still very much in love with this game of golf.

Truth be told, golf has always been his passion. It is why, in a roundabout way, he came to be such a key figure in local golf circles, because in the fall of 1950, Ezinicki wasn't in a hurry to show up at training camp with the Toronto Maple Leafs. The team had just won its third straight Stanley Cup, but Conn Smythe, the Toronto owner, hardly thought that excused his veteran right winger.

"He called me up and said, 'Bill, are you coming to camp?' " said Ezinicki. "I told him the snow hadn't started falling, that the golf courses were still open."

"Would you rather be playing hockey or on the golf course?" asked Smythe.

"I guess I'd rather be on the golf course," said Ezinicki, giving an answer that assured the 26-year-old winger a trip to Boston, traded along with Vic Lynn for Fern Flaman, Ken Smith, Phil Maloney, and Leo Boivin.

Boston? The kid from the outskirts of Winnipeg hardly knew a thing about the city. Oh, the hockey team he was familiar with. But did they have good golf courses?

"Then I remembered that the [US] Amateur champ had come from Boston [Ted Bishop, 1946], so I said to myself, 'They must have a lot of good golf courses.' "

Little did he know at the time that he would be one of the giants to walk those fairways.

For Ezinicki, hockey was not a sport growing up in Winnipeg in the 1930s; it was a way of life. "I just thought everyone played the game," he said.

Hockey appealed to him because it

didn't require great size, and he learned at a young age that if he could skate, he could play. He also discovered that with a full head of steam, he could hit hard in spite of his size, and that part of the game forever intrigued him.

From 1944 to 1950, Ezinicki was a Maple Leaf beloved in Toronto but hardly anywhere else. "Toronto has a leading candidate for the most hated opponent in Ezinicki," wrote longtime Boston Globe sports writer Herb Ralby after a game in which Ezinicki had flattened Boston goaltender Harry Lumley. But when Ezinicki donned the black-and-gold for the 1950-51 season, the viewpoint changed dramatically.

For two seasons, Ezinicki played for the Bruins, but he concedes that his interest in the game was waning by then. He was sold back to Toronto in 1952, then shipped to the Rangers for the 1954-55 season, which would be his last. At 32, he was now a golfer.

"He took his golf seriously," said former Bruins teammate Milt Schmidt. "More seriously, as a matter of fact, than hockey."

Ezinicki learned the game as a caddie, and long before it became chic for athletes to claim an affinity for golf, he studied its every nuance. In golf as in hockey, he found it mattered very little that he was small.

For several years after he retired from the NHL, Ezinicki tried his hand on the PGA Tour. The friendships he forged with legends such as Lawson Little and Dutch Harrison were special, but the travel was a grind and the money wasn't terrific. He had a handful of top-10 finishes, "and if he could have putted better, he would have made a lot more," said Harney, but truthfully Ezinicki knew his future was as a club pro. He worked at Colonial in Lynnfield, then got two terrific breaks: He was the first head pro named at New Seabury, and then he moved on to become the first head pro when The International opened in the early 1960s.

"When I came here [to The International] for the first time," said Ezinicki, "I looked around and said to myself, 'Thank God I got traded to Massachusetts.' Honest to God, that's how I felt. The people here have been so great to me."

And why not? You'd be hard-pressed to find a more engaging, genuine person than Ezinicki, whose playing accomplishments are a testimony to his greatness. In 1960 alone, he had a season that some would be grateful to call a career, with wins in four state opens — Massachusetts, Maine, New Hampshire, and Rhode Island. He added Vermont to that list in 1961, then won a second Mass. Open in 1964. Earlier, there had been two wins in the New England PGA Championship, plus his first of two New Hampshire Opens in 1958.

"He was mild-mannered; nothing ever upset him," said Harney, who played on the PGA Tour several summers with Ezinicki. "Had I done some of the things that I saw happen to him on the course, I'd have gotten upset. But things never fazed him."

Well, hardly ever.

"I remember taking a vacation once and going back to Winnipeg," said Ezinicki. "I got bit by one of those giant horseflies and I complained to my parents that I never get a vacation and here it got ruined. They looked at me and said, 'Who are you kidding? You've been on vacation all your life.'

"And you know what? They were right." ♀

Incredible drive

April 18, 2002 • By JIM McCABE

The sky over Hilton Head Island, South Carolina, was a warm, blue blanket. The ocean gently rolled to the nearby shore, then retreated in perfect rhythm. A small bird played a furious game of tag with a hawk, while a four-foot alligator crawled out from his small pond to rest in the warm grass beside the eighth fairway at Harbour Town Golf Links.

KIM JULIAN behind a photo of her late husband, Jeff.

"Could one that size hurt you?" Jeff Julian asked his caddie.

"Nah, too small," said Richard Hansberry. "Bogeys would hurt you more."

He nodded in agreement, then Julian continued his walk over the manicured, green fairway. He was playing golf, which was the most wonderful of all wonders on this dazzling day of sunshine. Julian was diagnosed in the fall of 2001 with amyotrophic lateral sclerosis (ALS), or, as it's more commonly called, Lou Gehrig's Disease.

The ALS had impaired his speech, but it didn't put a dent in his soul. Instead, it unleashed a human spirit that bore testament to all that is grand about life. And make no mistake, the Jeff Julian story is about life. It's about living with a determined dignity and profound love and appreciation for all that surrounds us.

Leaving the alligator to his rest, Julian walked to where his ball sat in the middle of the fairway. Having shaped his drive perfectly from right to left at the 470-yard, dogleg-left eighth, Julian had a mid-iron to the green. The swing was as it always has been — rhythmic, fluid, very few moving parts — and it wasn't hard to drift back to those days when Julian was growing up in Vermont and nurturing a love affair with this game called golf.

With an effortless grace, Julian made contact and delivered a shot that never left the pin, traveling a straight line for nearly 185 yards before coming to rest within 6 feet of the hole. His playing partners applauded heartily, as did the dozen or so folks in the gallery.

His smile warmer than the soft Carolina breeze, Julian gave a thumbs-up. Putting his arm around one of his amateur partners, Ron Reeves, Julian said, "It's great to be out here."

So why were people surprised at Julian's desire to keep playing golf? It's a game he played exquisitely for nearly a quarter century, a game that brought a joy that too many never find.

"I'd normally be doing this anyway," said Julian, sitting in glistening sunshine at one of the country's crown jewels of golf. "Look at this. How could you not be happy? I need this. I want this. And fortunately I have the chance to have it."

Julian was playing the PGA Tour this time on sponsor's exemptions. Earlier, there were berths at the AT&T Pebble Beach National Pro-Am, then the BellSouth Classic. In each case, he missed the cut, though the scores (77-78-74 and 74-76, respectively) are not a reflection of his physical condition, but rather of the way his golf career has gone: some days very good, others not so good.

He lost the 1994 New England Open in a playoff to Brett Quigley, but won the next year. He made it into three US Opens — 1990, 1995, 1996 — each time going through local and sectional qualifying. And he was there for two go-rounds on the PGA Tour, having made it through Q School twice.

Julian married Kimberly Young-blood in February 2001 and they were partners not only off the course, but on it as well, for she caddied in many of the PGA Tour events. They traveled to beautiful places, walked green fairways in warm breezes, and shared in the ups and downs of his game. Sometime around June, "we noticed he was slurring his words and his neck hurt," said Kimberly. By late summer, the concern had escalated and in October, a doctor at Johns Hopkins Hospital in Baltimore gave them the diagnosis: ALS, for which no cure is known.

"They basically give you some stuff to take and say, 'Here, go home and die,'" said Kimberly. But Jeff Julian couldn't think of giving up. Look at what he had done in golf.

The time he opened with an 82 at a Nike Tour event in 1997? He came back the next day and shot 63 to make the cut.

A short time later when an errant shot landed on a cart path and it looked like he was going to squander a chance to win the Dominion Open? Julian refused a free drop and played an incredible shot off the cart path, setting up a birdie and a one-shot win over Bobby Wadkins.

Q School at age 39, playing against the titanium kids and their 300-yard drives? Julian welcomed the challenge and earned membership to an exclusive club of superb golfers.

So he shrugged off the shock of the doctor's words and played on — even if it meant more treatments, medications, and understanding that the mere act of talking or eating put a strain on his neck muscles.

"Some of these guys out here only care about the money," said Hansberry, a caddie on Tour for parts of more than two dozen seasons. "But Jeff is such a great guy. I look at him and I say, 'I'm walking around and I'm complaining?'"

It's true. When the sky is blue, the fairways are green, and your mind has a permanent vision of Jeff Julian playing golf, all you can do is smile. ♀

Editor's Note: Jeff Julian died in the summer of 2004 in his beloved family farmhouse in Norwich, Vermont. He was 42.

if

Cuz Mingolla ever needed validation, he got it decades ago from Lee Trevino and Johnny Carson.

Chatting with Carson in the 1970s, Trevino told a national "Tonight Show" audience that life on the PGA Tour was terrific, and he praised places he had visited, such as Pleasant Valley Country Club in Sutton, Massachusetts.

Mingolla had built that humble course outside of Worcester in 1961 and then set out to bring professional golf to the area. There had been sporadic visits by notable pros in the past — Massachusetts Open winners included Gene Sarazen in 1935, Byron Nelson in 1939, Julius Boros in 1951 — but Mingolla wanted a consistent presence. In 1965, he saw his dream come true when Tony Lema won the Carling World Open at PV.

The stop at PV was an annual highlight to the New England sports calendar until it was discontinued in 1998. The roll call of champions included Arnold Palmer, Billy Casper, Raymond Floyd, Lanny Wadkins, George Archer, and Brad Faxon. For more than 30 years, New Englanders flocked to PV. But that isn't the only place where they showed their passion.

A PGA Tour stop had cropped up in Hartford, Connecticut, in 1952, and that, too, attracted big galleries. In 1980, the LPGA Tour began an 18-year run, first at Ferncroft Country Club in Danvers, Massachusetts, then down the road at Blue Hill Country Club in Canton. When senior golf for players over 50 became the rage, the Boston area got one of the first stops and today, the Bank of America Championship at Nashawtuc Country Club in Concord is the oldest 54-hole tournament on the Champions Tour.

Support of these pro golf stops was not surprising, for New Englanders had long expressed a love of the game and a fierce pride for the role the region played in its success. Mingolla's vision and commitment made sure the local thirst was quenched on a regular basis.

More recently, Seth Waugh has followed suit. Born and raised in Groton, Massachusetts, Waugh leveraged his position as CEO of Deutsche Bank in the Americas to help return the PGA Tour to his native state in 2003. The Deutsche Bank Championship features a fat purse ($7 million in 2007), fan passion, and a world-class field that has continued to charm us with great golf stories. —J.M.

Pleasant Valley roots run deep

September 9, 2001 • JIM McCABE

Brilliant sunshine has draped late-summer warmth over the landscape he cherishes, and when he stands upon the balcony of the clubhouse, Ted Mingolla sees nothing but green fairways and colorful flowers. Golf has been his life, and like all of those who are avid about the game, he understands this is the best time of year. The weather is ideal and the course conditions are at their peak.

Tucked away in the Central Massachusetts town of Sutton, Pleasant Valley Country Club has always offered great golf, from wonderfully played New England PGA Championships to a recent amateur four-ball that was decided with a birdie on the 54th hole. That pleases Mingolla, who owns this country club that was the product of his father's sweat and blood.

Cuz Mingolla brought more professional golf to the area than anyone else, and his son did a good job keeping it going.

Mickey Wright in 1964. Tony Lema in 1965. Kathy Whitworth in 1966, then again in '67, '69, and '71. Arnold Palmer in 1968. Billy Casper in 1970. Ray Floyd in 1977. Brad Faxon in 1992. Pretty good names to have on your roll call of champions, and the list of winners at Pleasant Valley stretches on and on. Dozens of times the PGA Tour stopped by. And there were numerous visits by the LPGA Tour, too.

All of which makes September a bittersweet time for Mingolla. For many years, the weekend after Labor Day was PGA Tour time at Pleasant Valley, and he concedes he misses the excitement, the tens of thousands of spectators, the special friendships he had with players such as Lee Trevino, Curtis Strange, Fuzzy Zoeller, Joey Sindelar, and Paul Azinger.

"It was part of the fabric here," said Mingolla. "It was a lot of work and for many years it was a money-losing proposition, but we loved it."

And now that several PGA Tour seasons have passed without stops at PV — tossing aside a history that dates back to 1965 — Mingolla doesn't mince words.

"We're still bitter about how the Tour pulled the rug out from under us," he said, "mostly for the great golf fans who supported us for years."

Mingolla knows the landscape of the PGA Tour has changed a lot over the years. In the old days, his dad used to pick up players at Boston's Logan Airport, and in Mingolla's early days in charge, getting Azinger's motor home hooked up with electricity was part of his job — one of the many personal touches that made the experience special.

"Then it all became so corporate, so complex," said Mingolla. "Courtesy cars. Demands. It changed. It was awful, and a lot of that I don't miss."

Mingolla even admits that his sometimes stubborn nature contributed to problems with commissioner Deane Beman, then with Beman's successor, Tim Finchem.

"I was president of the American Golf Sponsors Association," said Mingolla. "I was their mouth, mostly because I owned my own course, I guess, and they thought I'd fight for us."

Which he did. Sometimes to his own detriment.

Beman suggested the PGA Tour buy Pleasant Valley and turn it into a TPC course, but Mingolla balked. Sponsors were always tough to find, and Mingolla said he didn't get any help from the PGA Tour. For four years, the event was called the Pleasant Valley Classic, twice it was the Pleasant Valley Jimmy Fund Classic, and for four summers it was simply the New England Classic.

"We ran it ourselves," said Mingolla. "Was it a good business decision to keep having that tournament? It was not, but we got great crowds and people were happy. We kept hoping for the best."

He knows the fields were sometimes thin, but still the people came, as many as 50,000 to 60,000 some Sundays. He's got great memories and doesn't hesitate to mention Azinger, who won in 1993 and was diagnosed with cancer a few months later.

"There was a year when he could have gotten $30,000 to play in Belgium, but he turned it down to play here," said Mingolla. "He appreciated what we had done for him."

Zoeller? Mingolla laughs. He used to provide transportation to a private hunting and fishing reserve "because Zoeller was such a nut about that stuff."

The best tournament? "[Bruce] Fleisher's win over [Ian] Baker-Finch in 1991," said Mingolla, citing their seven-hole playoff. The unheralded Fleisher beat the rising star from Australia.

As for Mingolla, the tournament provided a lot of exposure for Pleasant Valley, and its status as a great "family club" is owed in some part to those many years of PGA Tour stops.

And for New England fans? "I'd like to think we offered them 32 great years of golf."

Two for the road

September 1, 2005 • By JIM McCABE

The practice range at TPC Boston was end-to-end with golfers who'd made it to the PGA Tour in a variety of ways. They'd come from Australia and India, Sweden and South Africa, to play in the 2005 Deutsche Bank Championship. They were household names and unheralded journeymen. They were rich and not-so-rich, all vying for a $5.5 million purse.

the right time," Sean O'Hair said of his wife. "She always believed that I would make it out here [on the PGA Tour]."

Maybe not this quickly — could anyone have predicted that Sean, while still in his early 20s, would rocket from playing minitour golf to earning millions of dollars at PGA events? — but yes, Jackie O'Hair believed. And the route the couple put all their faith in wound from their home outside of

could be playing on the [LPGA] Tour if she wanted," said Sean.

Jackie's family became Sean's family. Their home became Sean's home. And after Sean and Jackie were married, it was agreed that the summer of 2003 would best be spent playing the Cleveland Golf Tour, a series of 10 events that began in early June. He'd play, she'd caddie.

"It wasn't about location and it wasn't about being comfortable," said Sean. "It was about the competition. The Cleveland Golf Tour offered great competition."

To prepare for the competition, the O'Hairs invested in a truck with a cover that stretched over the back, beneath which they kept their belongings stored in bins.

Needless to say, Waikiki Beach is a long way from Nauset Beach.

And then there was Sean O'Hair, whose story was perhaps the feel-good bonanza of them all.

We'd heard about the boy groomed to be a superstar by an overzealous father; his years at a specialized golf academy; the tactics used to get the most out of the kid; the decision to forgo a normal high school experience, never mind college, and chase the grueling pro golf life at the tender age of 17; the slap-in-the-face realities brought on by failure; and the painful breaking point when son and father became estranged.

If the story had ended there, it would be like so many others, but romance rewrote the script. Tragic became brilliant, all because of Jackie O'Hair.

"It was meant to be. She's my guardian angel. She came around at

Philadelphia via Interstate 95 to New England, where Sean O'Hair made his mark on the Cleveland Golf Tour — a minitour circuit that he may no longer need, but will always owe.

"I looked at all the minitours and it was the best-run of them all. No one was better," said O'Hair. "I'll never forget [tour founder] Brian Hebb and everything he did for me. Getting to the PGA Tour is all about being prepared, and the Cleveland Golf Tour prepared me."

Estranged from his father after a few aimless years as a teenage professional, O'Hair found Jackie Lucas at a golf course in South Florida. Their first "date," if you will, was a round of golf, and the young lady who had played at Florida International impressed the young pro.

"There's no doubt in my mind she

"We'd get back from the golf course and we'd all be staying at the same hotel, and we'd watch them unload their Rubbermaid bins," said Andrew Dearborn, tour director for the CGT. "They had the plates, the hot plates, all their dishes — everything they needed. It was kind of neat."

"We cooked chicken, a lot of Hamburger Helper, all sorts of stuff," Sean remembered. "It was cheaper, but while money was definitely an issue, we liked being together. There are a lot of good memories."

Perhaps highest on the list is Sean's first win, at Blackstone National in Sutton, Massachusetts, a victory that Dearborn suggests was career-altering. "The first thing I remember about Sean is how good a swing he had. He looked like a strong player and always was challenging the top players. But that win put him in another level."

The O'Hairs enjoyed all flavors of New England that summer, the mountains of Vermont and New Hampshire, the rocky coast of Maine, the small towns of Massachusetts. They both agreed that the tournament at Captains Golf Course in Brewster, Massachusetts, was their favorite.

"Nauset Beach? We loved it," said Jackie O'Hair.

"Just to chill out, to be together," said Sean. "It wasn't like work; it was like a vacation where we'd do a little work."

Then they got the motorhome.

"It was a 2003 Fleetwood Discovery, a 40-footer," said Sean O'Hair, whose father's parents bought it for them.

"We'd always look for a Wal-Mart [parking lot]," said Jackie. "They were nice enough to allow you to stay overnight."

Some days he finished tied for 17th and took home a check for $187. But if it occurred to him that this was no way to make a living, Jackie refused to let him ponder that for long. Even when she became pregnant and they decided she shouldn't caddie, she remained his faithful copilot in the motorhome.

People began to take notice when Sean won a tournament at Sterling Country Club. Then, before they knew it, he was the CGT's leading money-winner, talented enough to set his sights on Marshfield's Geoff Sisk, the perennial Player of the Year and a guy who'd made the cut at the US Open.

"Geoff spent a lot of time with him," said Hebb. "He helped mentor him."

"But I would tell him, 'Don't be focused on just me,'" said Sisk. "Just go out and play your best."

SEAN O'HAIR AND TIGER WOODS work the back nine of the Tournament Players Club of Boston during a 2005 Deutsche Bank Championship practice round.

For most of the summer of 2005, O'Hair's best made him the leading money-winner, but then Sisk put on a mistake-free performance at Samoset to take the money title. And O'Hair didn't let it get him down.

In his sixth try at the annual grind known as the PGA Tour Qualifying Tournament — at the tender age of 22, no less — O'Hair never shot higher than 72 and finished tied for fourth. Less than five weeks later, he was playing in his first PGA Tour event, the Sony Open in Hawaii, a fashionable way to begin his rookie season.

Needless to say, Waikiki Beach is a long way from Nauset Beach, and the O'Hairs still shake their heads over a subsequent win at the John Deere Classic, a whirlwind trip to St. Andrews for the British Open, and more than $2 million earned in a season that delivered Rookie of the Year honors.

The motorhome has been sold, and now when they travel from Philadelphia to New England for a golf tournament, they fly. It's a sign of how things have changed, but Jackie O'Hair will never forget those times when they meandered through New England.

"This is the dream he worked so hard and so long for," she said. "He deserves it." ⛳

byron nelson

> *"I don't care if he was playing against orangutans, winning 11 straight is amazing."*

BYRON NELSON
and stepson
John Tangeman
at Ponkapoag.

Lord Byron drops in

September 17, 1998 • By JIM McCABE

The swing that rarely failed him, so automatic and so fluid, was a distant memory, but the dignity that had defined his life was very much present. Even in his 80s, Byron Nelson, the ultimate gentleman, still had a passion for golf.

"I love the game, love to be around it," he said that day in 1998. "Always have, ever since I first played when I was 13."

The man affectionately called Lord Byron graced the New England golf landscape as a visitor to Ponkapoag Golf Course in Canton, Massachusetts, where his stepson, John Tangeman, was a member. Had it not been for an accident in his woodworking shop, Nelson would have teed it up, as he has in other visits; instead, his left thumb wrapped in a bandage thanks to 16 stitches, he was content to reminisce, to answer questions, to watch his stepson play golf.

"Does he ask you for advice?" Nelson was asked.

"Of course. Oh, sure he does," said Nelson. "But he plays pretty well."

Polite praise from a man who spent his life around this game; a man who at one time came closer than anyone to doing the impossible: playing perfect golf. It was 1945. Between March 8 and August 4 Nelson won every tournament he entered — 11 straight. No one has come close and it is doubtful anyone ever will.

Nelson agrees, but he is so very humble, he says the record will survive not because the players aren't good enough, but because the sports world in 1998 is far different from 1945. "There's so much pressure today," said Nelson. "I feel sorry for Tiger Woods. I really do. He needs an escort to get to the practice tee. Peter Jacobsen won two straight tournaments a couple of years ago and he told me, 'I don't know how you did it. The pressure is already getting to me.'

"But it never bothered me. Golf wasn't that big back then. When I won the Masters in 1937, I went to the locker room and there was one reporter."

There are those who will try to discredit Nelson's incredible feat and tell you the competition was thin, that the war years took some great players (Ben Hogan in particular) away from the Tour. To those cynics, there is only one response, and it came from Jackie Burke years ago, after he had won four straight Tour stops, the closest anyone has come to matching Nelson: "I don't care if he was playing against orangutans, winning 11 straight is amazing."

Equally incredible is the fact that Nelson, a year removed from 11 straight wins and 18 in the season, called it quits, retiring at 34 to a ranch just north of Fort Worth that is still home. "I had set goals in my mind. I decided it was important to win all the major tournaments — the 1939 US Open, two Masters, two PGAs — and I had done that. But I didn't make any money."

So he became a cattle farmer and lived happily away from the rigors of travel and competition. But he never really left the game of golf, for which the sport should be entirely grateful. We know Ken Venturi is. So, too, Tom Watson. And Phil Mickelson makes three pros who owe many thanks to the quiet gentleman who has walked with golf's giants, from Bobby Jones to Tiger Woods.

Forever, though, Nelson will be linked with Hogan. They grew up in Fort Worth, caddied at the same course, got into pro golf around the same time, and for many years they and Sam Snead made up the sport's greatest trio, each so very different. Hogan was the recluse, Snead flamboyant, Nelson the consummate gentleman. While they were not the closest of friends, Nelson and Hogan shared moments that will live forever in golf folklore, the most famous being their Masters playoff in 1942 (Nelson won).

For Nelson, another significant memory was his 1939 playoff loss to Henry Picard in the PGA Championship: "I was 1-up and put a chip shot to about 3 feet on the 36th hole. Picard knocked it to about a foot, absolutely stymied me. Now I'm trying to be as honest as possible, though losers always exaggerate."

And then there was the 1937 British Open: "I finished fourth and won $187. It cost me $3,000 to make that trip and take a month off from my job at a club in Reading, Pennsylvania."

And finally, Nelson laughed while recalling the 1939 Massachusetts Open at Worcester Country Club, where his good friend, Harold "Jug" McSpaden, was the head pro: "The only reason he invited me was because it was his home course and he figured he could beat me." But McSpaden came up short, again.

Nelson didn't meet with a lot of fanfare during his career, and not much of a fuss was made on the occasion of his appearance at Ponkapoag in 1998, either.

A few women two fairways over yelled out their best wishes and some gentlemen stopped by to meet him. He smiled, shook hands, and somehow conveyed that the honor was his.

True legends are like that. ♀

Editor's Note: Byron Nelson died in September of 2006. He was 94.

STYLISH PRACTITIONERS on this page are (l-r from top row) Dana Quigley, Keith Orien, Charlie Volpone (again), Jennifer Rosales, Douglas Preston, Brad Faxon, Michelle Bell, and Colleen Walker. At far right is Brian Quinn with his caddie; and on page 141, Andrew Morse gets the eye from his caddie/wife, Sue.

139

Plumb crazy pros

August 30, 2005 • By JIM McCABE

Left edge, right edge, three balls out. Inside left, inside right, there's never a doubt.

The late, great Dr. Seuss could have used that in a book on the art of plumb-bobbing to read a putt. Certainly, it would have been perfect fodder for his sense of humor, for when it comes to questions about plumb-bobbing — the technique for reading a putt by standing behind your ball and holding your putter vertically in front of your eyes — most people don't have a clue.

"I watch guys do it all the time and they're doing it wrong," said Lee Janzen, a faithful plumb-bobber. "They don't know what they're doing."

Janzen certainly can't be talking about Chris Smith, because the 2002 Buick Classic champion has never gone through the routine in his pro career. In fact, said Smith, "I had two brothers and they were high school and college age and they decided you had to plumb-bob. So they were trying to teach me how to plumb-bob and I did it for two days and decided it was the biggest waste of time."

Smith laughed, as did Billy Andrade when he remembered the one time he ever plumb-bobbed in a PGA Tour event. It came years ago at a stop in Houston "and I had played with these guys in the pro-am who were plumb-bobbing," said Andrade. "I told them, 'You guys don't have a clue what you're doing.' So when I got to the 18th hole on Sunday, I saw them sitting up in the stands and I decided to plumb-bob this 20-footer I had and they just laughed."

The putt?

"I missed it," said Andrade. "Plumb-bobbing is overrated."

That's not a sentiment shared by a couple of Andrade's pals from the Rhode Island golf fraternity, because joining Janzen on the plumb-bobbing bandwagon are Dana Quigley and his brother Paul. To them, learning to plumb-bob — the term comes from a lead weight that is used as a crude level — is as essential as learning to keep drives under the Ocean State breezes.

"I plumb-bob all my putts and plumb-bob all of Dana's and all of Brett's putts, too," said Paul Quigley, a multiple winner of the Rhode Island State Amateur who has caddied for son Brett on the PGA Tour. "It's the way I grew up."

And you, Dana?

"Absolutely. I do it on every putt. It gives you an indication [of the break], but, of course, nothing is absolute," said the frequent Champions Tour winner. "If you don't know what you're doing, you'll only confuse yourself."

Enter, please, a Stanford graduate to shed light on all of this. Notah Begay, your feelings on plumb-bobbing?

"I think it is extremely overrated in terms of the physics concept called parallax," said Begay. "Most people don't understand the concept. A lot of them never took a physics course. But, if you're totally lost, it definitely can help."

Parallax? A Google search comes up with explanations such as, "the vision effect of having two eyes viewing the same scene from slightly different positions that creates a sense of depth." But the players put it in their own words. They talk about the need to let the shaft hang straight ("the toe faces toward you," said Ben Crenshaw) and not blow in the wind, then you close whatever eye isn't your dominant one ("I think that's my left one," said Brad Faxon) and you line the shaft of the putter directly over the ball and "if it's left of the hole," said Paul Quigley, "the ball will break left-to-right."

Maybe.

"Remember, it not an exact science; it's only an indicator," said Crenshaw, whose putting prowess was most evident when he twice won the Masters. But Crenshaw concedes that plumb-bobbing on severe slopes like those at Augusta is not necessary. "When the break is straightforward, you don't need to," he said. "It's best when done on flatter surfaces, or when you have the appearance of a flat surface."

On that point, devout disciples of plumb-bobbing are in agreement. But Smith, for one, isn't about to start plumb-bobbing on any surface, flat or not flat.

"Just by looking at guys doing it and knowing and listening to what they're doing, it's way too much information for me," said Smith. "It confuses me."

And even Faxon says it's a tool to be used sparingly. "Really, I don't plumb-bob a lot because I don't think it reads enough break into the putt," he explained.

Perhaps, said Begay, that's because it's impossible to keep the shaft completely still, which is essential to get a true plumb-bob. Begay's degree is in economics, but he didn't sleep through those physics lectures; he knows how plumb-bobbing works.

"In terms of gravity and gravitational pull, I do," he said. "I understand the concept. But I don't think it fits me."

Nor does it seem to fit his collegiate teammate, for Tiger Woods doesn't plumb-bob, either. Instead, he stalks a putt from every angle, and if you think he's simply figuring out the putt with his eyes, think again. Woods is using that part of his body that many golfers say relays the most crucial information: the feet.

"I pay more attention to my feet than my eyes," said Smith. "It's why I always walk halfway to the hole from where my ball is, especially late in the day when it's hard to see."

Janzen relies on his feet, too, but he falls back on plumb-bobbing for confirmation. Crenshaw understands, committed plumb-bobber that he is.

"It's a second look, certainly, it's a crutch, no doubt about it," said Crenshaw, who used the technique as far back as his amateur days when he played in the Northeast Amateur at Wannamoisett in Rumford, Rhode Island.

Paul Quigley was at those events and remembers watching Crenshaw stand tall behind his ball and hold up his putter to plumb-bob. Quigley figured if it was good enough for Crenshaw, it would be good enough for him, though his own son has never done it, nor have many of the players for whom he has caddied.

"I was doing it one day for Hank Kuehne," said Paul Quigley. "He looked at me and said, 'Paul, I don't want to know how to do it. All I want to know is, is it left or is it right?' " ⚑

TIPS (SORT OF)

OK, so let's hurdle the confusion and simply explain how you go about plumb-bobbing.

1 THOSE WHO DO IT AGREE THAT YOU MUST STAND DIRECTLY BEHIND THE BALL ...

• *I've heard that you should stand whatever your height is away from your ball, but I generally stand 6 to 10 feet behind the ball.* PAUL QUIGLEY

• *But you need to straddle the line, I think.* BRAD FAXON

2 SO, ONCE YOU FIGURE OUT WHERE TO STAND, YOU HOLD UP A PUTTER ...

• *I use a wedge, but only because Brett always is already holding the putter.* PAUL QUIGLEY,

3 OK, YOU HOLD UP A WEDGE OR A PUTTER ...

• *But the trouble is, that a lot of putters you can't do it with because they're not face-balanced or heel-balanced. They move too much. I see guys doing it with the wrong putters all the time.* LEE JANZEN

4 ALL RIGHT, SO THE TRICK IS TO GET A WEDGE OR THE RIGHT PUTTER, AND LINE IT UP OVER THE BALL, THEN ...

• *I know most players (close one eye), but I always keep both eyes opened ... I see two shafts, the real one and the transparent one. I look for what's on the inside edge of the transparent one.* BEN CRENSHAW

5 BUT IF YOU DO CLOSE ONE EYE?

• *You're looking at the cup to get a perspective of how far to start the ball out to have it end up at the hole. The putter will have a balance point, so you look up the shaft and you see an area left or right of the hole.* PAUL QUIGLEY

6 EITHER WAY, THE THING TO DO NOW IS ...

Putt, already.

The greatest golfer ever?

September 5, 2006 •

By JACKIE MacMULLAN

It was over after three holes.

I know what the scoreboard of the 2006 Deutsche Bank Championship in Norton, Massachusetts, said. The final results were that Tiger Woods beat Vijay Singh by two strokes to walk off with his fifth straight tournament victory. Those numbers suggest a battle of epic proportions between two of the world's most decorated golfers.

But here's the flaw in that story line: Woods, who began the final round three strokes off the lead, made up all three on the first three holes. In other words, it took him just one-sixth of his round to completely wipe out the advantage his opponent had systematically assembled the previous day with a course-record score of 61.

I don't care who you are. That's demoralizing, particularly when it's Tiger laying down the hammer.

In fact, just to make sure he totally annihilated any momentum Singh might have mustered, Woods continued his assault by shooting 6 under par on the front nine. And it could have easily been 8 under had he not missed a pair of birdie putts that were off by the width of a blade of grass.

Thus, when Woods and Singh turned the corner to approach the 10th tee, Tiger, who was supposed to be chasing Vijay, was, in fact, enjoying a three-shot lead.

Really now. Who is supposed to be able to withstand that kind of attack? Not Singh, who had won 29 PGA Tour tournaments (including this one two years ago by topping Woods) and in Tiger's words "is one of the most

tiger woods

consistent players on our tour, one of the most consistent players in the world."

To his credit, Singh hardly wilted under the pressure. He has been here before, he knows what it entails, and that's why he was able to hang around and prevent Tiger from simply running off with another victory.

It's just that Tiger woke up intent on winning this tournament. And when he is wearing his trademark flaming red, come-and-get-me final-day shirt, not to mention his Darth Vader death stare, it's hard to make up ground.

The fact that Woods was able to wrap up this particular item on his "to do" list (No. 1, win my own tournament; No. 2, bring home milk) with such fervor and concentration surprised even the master himself.

"I hit it good," Woods said, in what can only be described as an under-statement.

By the time he dropped in a 25-foot putt for birdie on 17, Woods was swinging freely, and with the ease of a champion.

A champion who might someday equal the great Byron Nelson, who won a record 11 straight tournaments in 1945?

"You'd have to have so many things go right," said Woods. "To win 11 in a row in this day and age with the competition [we have] would almost be unheard of.

"What Byron accomplished goes down as one of the greatest streaks in all of sport. I don't know about [Joe] DiMaggio's record [56-game hitting streak]. I see that being broken sooner than winning 11 golf tournaments."

But, Tiger, is it doable?

"It's doable if a lot of guys pull out," he deadpanned.

You wonder if it matters. His favorite opponent appears to be himself and he's beating him, too. ♀

A parent sets priorities

August 27, 2003 • By JIM McCABE

It was big news when Tiger Woods, after seven years as a pro, made his first appearance in New England in a PGA Tour event known as the Deutsche Bank Championship, held at TPC Boston in 2003. But almost as significant was the fact that his father also made the trip, for so much of the Tiger Woods legend was molded by Earl and Kultida Woods.

Though an avid follower of his son's exploits on the golf course, Earl Woods could have followed the proceedings quite comfortably from his home in Southern California. He didn't make this coast-to-coast journey just to watch Tiger play golf. He came because he was president of the Tiger Woods Foundation and proceeds of the tournament stood to benefit that organization.

"Golf is important to [Tiger]," said Earl Woods before the tournament, "but other things are important to me. I don't even think about golf except when Tiger's playing. We're going to make a difference. We need to help inner-city kids. We want to give them the opportunity to start to dream again. We want to empower them to be the best they can be."

Earl Woods agreed to emcee a junior golf clinic at TPC Boston because helping youngsters was so much a part of him. The legend of Eldrick Woods, after all, began when Earl's son was a junior golfer, and the tales from those many years ago are part of the game's lore.

⌐ How Earl named his son Eldrick "Tiger" after a Vietnamese soldier, Vuong Dang Phong, he befriended during the Vietnam War.

⌐ How Earl would take golf swings in front of his infant son, knowing children learn by repetition.

⌐ How Earl brought Tiger to Navy Golf Club in their hometown of Cypress, California, and the kid shot 48 for nine holes — at the age of 3.

Earl was there every step of the way in the development of Tiger Woods, but he insisted it was never his intention to be the father of the greatest golfer ever.

"My objective," he said, "was to make Tiger a good person. Tiger was going to have success in whatever endeavor he chose. He chose golf. I didn't choose golf for him. He plays for himself."

Still, Earl Woods could spot his son's gift for a game that he himself had always been pretty good at. So if the kid was going to devote so much passion and energy toward it, the retired Army lieutenant colonel figured he and Kultida had to be involved. There had to be rules. There had to be a sense of responsibility. There was no guidebook to tell them how to go about it, so they felt their way along the junior golf circuit, all the while insisting that their son keep up his studies.

He never failed them on that count, so they never denied him the opportunity to play a national junior golf schedule. It just had to be done in moderation, and in fact Earl Woods bemoaned what has happened to the intense junior golf scene in this country. He authored several books about his early years with his son, sharing his thoughts on how parents should handle things. "But I can't force people to read," he said. "It isn't the kids. I don't know what's up with these parents. They see the kids as a gold mine at the end of the tunnel."

His son played an aggressive junior schedule, yes. But what people often forget is that Earl would force

Tiger to put the clubs down for a few weeks after a two-, or three-, or four-week run.

"Go ride your bike or play Nintendo or goof off. Have a childhood," Earl would say to Tiger. "He'd tell me he was pooped, tired of golf and the first day he'd ride his bike over to his friend's house. Then the second day he'd ride his bike. Then the third day he'd pick up the clubs and he'd walk around the house, dribbling the ball on the clubface like everyone's seen him do.

"He'd dribble that ball over the house. Then he'd walk around the living room and start hitting these little shots over the chandelier, over the coffee table, cute little shots. He'd make the ball stop, then suck it back right before it got to the fireplace. His mother saw it and said, 'You better not break anything.' You talk about pressure? That was pressure."

The next day, Tiger would be begging to play, and Earl's lesson was clear. "It had to be his decision, not mine."

There was the time young Tiger hit an awful shot in a junior tournament at Lake Nona, Florida, and Earl Woods laughed from the side of the fairway. Tiger saw him laugh, then shortly thereafter hit another awful shot. Again, the father laughed and again the son glared.

"Later, he said to me, 'Why were you laughing at me?' And I told him, 'Son, I was trying to tell you something. Golf is a game. Enjoy it and have fun. Besides, you're not that good.'"

Earl Woods believed in such lessons. He was asked about sending junior players into competition against PGA Tour players — specifically the sponsor's exemptions a young Michelle Wie accepted to play against men — and he shook his head.

"I never entered Tiger in a tournament in which he was outmanned," said Earl. "Every one I entered him into, I felt he had to have a chance to win. I didn't want him to lose confidence."

The record supports him here, because there has never been a junior golfer any better, any more prepared than Tiger Woods, yet he never played a pro event until he was 16.

Speaking to the junior golf picture in general, Earl Woods said, "I use the word 'push' here. [Parents] are pushing too fast. Literally."

He remembered the 1992 day at Franklin Park in Dorchester, Massachusetts, when his son, then playing in the US Junior Amateur at nearby Wollaston Golf Club, thrilled a large throng of youngsters with a clinic.

Tiger Woods was just 16 at the time, but there was no mistaking the aura. There still isn't.

"He has the power to do a lot of things with his charisma," said Earl Woods. "Someday, he will do a lot of great things. I don't know what they are yet, but knowing Tiger Woods, they won't be small." ⚲

Editor's Note: Earl Woods died of prostate cancer in May of 2006.

> ## *"I told him ... Golf is a game. Enjoy it and have fun. Besides, you're not that good."*

Still carrying a torch

August 30, 2006 • By JIM McCABE

What you see is the heavy golf bag that they whip over their shoulders and strap to their backs. What you don't see is the passion that burns within them for this game of golf.

They are caddies, yes; but so, too, are many of them players who once dreamed of life in the big leagues. Some still do.

"There are a lot of really good players among the caddies, guys who have put their careers on hold," said Robert Ames, who caddies for his brother, Stephen.

He hasn't given up on his dream, not totally, so Robert Ames tries to find time to play whenever possible, including teaming with Stephen as the Trinidad-and-Tobago entry in multiple World Cups. But, as he said, "to try and carry this thing around and try and play is very tough."

Robert Ames is not the only caddie with his own competitive playing schedule. "I still love to compete," said Scott Tway, who caddies for Scott Verplank after working for years with his brother, Bob. In fact, it was at his brother's insistence that Scott Tway would enter minitour tournaments between PGA Tour stops. "He wanted me to remember how hard it was, just to keep good perspective," said Scott.

Walk up and down the range or stroll past the caddie shack at any weekly PGA Tour stop and you'll see them assembled, usually within arm's length of their man's golf bag. Much of their time is spent standing and waiting, the most important rule being to be ready that split-second they're asked to move. So often the caddies blend into the landscape, bit players on a stage dominated by the guys who swing the clubs and make the shots. But many can point to a time when they were the ones who did the playing.

Lance Ten Broeck, who loops for Jesper Parnevik, played in 349 PGA Tour events over a career that stretched from 1975-98. He made the cut 159 times, recorded 10 top-10 finishes and was good enough to finish second in the 1991 Chattanooga Classic. (As a true indicator of how you never know in this game, the guy who finished third that year is a PGA Tour legend, John Daly, and the champion, Dillard Pruitt, is a PGA Tour rules official.)

Then there's Damon Green, who is perhaps the best player among the caddies. A big man with a quiet demeanor, Green works for Zach Johnson, but in another lifetime he was his own boss, a minitour legend of sorts, with 64 wins to his credit. In 1995-96, Green was fully exempt on the Nationwide Tours, but after 51 tournaments and only a little more than $30,000 in prize money, he faced that moment of truth that so many competitive golfers do.

"I felt like it was the end of the road as a player," said Green. "But I didn't really know what else to do. I didn't really want to be a head pro. I didn't want to stand behind a desk and teach for those enormous amount of hours."

He was friends with Scott Hoch and Fulton Allem, then regular members of the PGA Tour, and with Jimmy Green, who had Nationwide Tour status, so he accepted offers to caddie. When Hoch phoned him and offered the bag full time, Damon Green told him he'd have to think about it, "even though at the same time I was on the phone jumping up and down."

> ## "To try and carry this thing around and try and play is very tough."

If there's a common denominator in caddies, that is it: They love the game.

"If you don't, you're in trouble," said one of the game's best, Andy Martinez. He's been looping for too many years to remember, and if there was a time in his younger life when he thought he may have been able to be a serious player, that idea was dispelled by his boss.

"Johnny Miller," said Martinez, "took the fun out of the game for me." Miller was clearly superior in every facet of the game. It was beautiful to watch, said Martinez, but also humbling.

For some caddies, the decision to give up playing is more of a personal struggle.

"Everybody's different," said Billy

Heim, who caddies for former PGA Championship winner Rich Beem. "For me, this job seemed a little more stable, more enjoyable and the guy I work for is fantastic. I had hit a road-block. I felt like I wasn't getting any better; that's why I stopped playing."

Mike "Fluff" Cowan said he figured things out early enough in his career to spare him the long, grinding life that pro golf can be. Having grown up in Maine, he turned pro but had a short-lived career as a player. He was

there long enough, however, to come away with a golden view of things.

"The only way to get better," said Cowan, "is to compete."

Scott Tway still subscribes to that notion, which is why he takes note of Nationwide Monday qualifiers whenever he's in town. It's why Robert Ames searches for matches in which to tune his game. And it's why Ten Broeck, your onetime Vermont Open champion, has tried the Champions Tour Q School and Monday qualifiers

on the European PGA Senior Tour.

They are caddies first, but still they have some player in them. ⚲

SOME GOLF LOVERS get a free ride (below), while others carry the load. Pictured on pages 146-147 (clockwise from left) are David Gossett with caddie Andy Martinez, Vijay Singh with caddie Scott Brady, and a caddie shack full of Bay State youngsters awaiting work at the Winchester Country Club.

dana quigley

A league of his own

June 21, 2001 • By JIM McCABE

Billboards and bright lights were a blur as he cruised along Interstate 95 that February night in South Florida. Dana Quigley was a man in a hurry, so he drove fast, but the faster he drove, the more the billboards and bright lights melted into something resembling a tunnel.

He knew where he had come from, but wondered how he'd gotten there. He knew where he was going, but wondered why he was going.

So he stopped.

"I just pulled the car off the highway, turned it right around at the exit, and went home," he said. "I just knew I was going to end up either killing myself or, worse than that, killing some poor, innocent person in another car and end up in jail."

Just like that, Quigley bid farewell to a part of his life that had helped define who he was. Hard-living, fun-loving Dana Quigley, a tell-it-like-it-is type of guy who happened to think that playing golf and then throwing down a few beers was the perfect way to spend a day. Every day.

"I was three-quarters lit, on the way to a restaurant to drink some more," said Quigley of that February night in 1990. "At the exit, it hit me. For some reason, it dawned on me."

Eventually there would be some professional help, some counseling. But the first step, the one that is so difficult for alcoholics to take, he made himself.

"I woke up the next morning and decided I wasn't going to drink again," said Quigley. "And I haven't had a drink since then."

Years later, in the lunchroom at Ridgewood Country Club in Paramus, New Jersey, Quigley sat with Ed Dougherty, one of his best friends on Tour, and Paul Parajeckas, the head pro from Woburn Country Club in Massachusetts. Quigley's lunch that day in 2001 consisted of macaroni salad, cole slaw, and two bags of potato chips. Standing nearby, another old friend laughed. "The club pro's lunch," said the man. "Grab something quick, get to the tee. He's still a club pro at heart."

Except that he has a touring pro's lifestyle now: private jets, courtesy cars, corporate outings, national exposure, and a weekly chance to win tens and hundreds of thousands of dollars.

"My God, every day is like Disney

> *"My God, every day is like Disney World."*

World," said Quigley, quickly finishing his second bag of potato chips.

In his sport today, players talk about needing time off after playing three or four straight weeks, how they need to put the clubs away and get away from it. Not Quigley.

"I used to drive from Rhode Island to Maine to play for $5,000 purses," he said. "You think I'm going to give up the chance to play for $1 million?"

Always, Dana Quigley could play. In the wind, in the rain, in the stifling heat, it didn't matter. The guy from Rhode Island could play. Everyone knew it.

"He was always a huge talent," said Paul Quigley, two years older than his brother. "And he had passion for the game."

"I'd watch him hit balls all the time at Rhode Island Country Club," said Brad Faxon. "He had a presence about him. He was tall, good-looking, and always dressed nice. I looked up to him and watched the way he carried himself."

"This was a guy who had been out there," said Billy Andrade. "He had played on Tour. You had to respect that."

Indeed, Quigley had tested his talents against the best in his younger years. Shortly after graduating from the University of Rhode Island in 1969, he turned pro, gave PGA Tour School a shot, but failed. He went through a series of club jobs until the bug bit him again, in the fall of 1977. This time, he shocked himself and made it.

"I don't know what even led me to try it," he said. "Just on a whim."

From 1978-1982, Quigley toured the country. These were the days before the all-exempt Tour, when there were plenty of spots available for Monday qualifiers. In his bell-bottoms and long hair, Quigley always played well enough to keep his playing privileges, just not well enough to crack through.

The PGA Tour then, as now, was no place for someone who didn't feel he belonged. And no matter how much game he had, no matter how many Monday qualifiers he made, Dana Quigley couldn't quite overcome his belief that he did not belong on Tour.

"I remember back then I used to go to the range and hide," said Quigley.

"It was tough to play like that."

Back in his comfort zone, the New England PGA, Quigley became head pro at Crestwood Country Club in Rehoboth and from 1983-1996 he dominated the competition. He won state opens in Massachusetts, Rhode Island, and Vermont, virtually lived atop leaderboards, and nailed down NEPGA Player of the Year honors seven times. In 1986, he was third in the national Club Professional Championship.

They were great days, said Quigley. Sometimes too good.

"The drinking was part of our being. We weren't drunks because we needed the feeling. We were just social, very social guys. We went out and had a good time. It was the whole deal."

"Hey, I've never had a drink in my life, not a taste," said Paul Quigley, "but I knew that unless he was ready to give it up, it didn't matter what anyone said. Dana can be very stubborn. You say something's black and he'll argue."

There was no arguing that February night in 1990 when he decided to quit drinking. Nor was there any fanfare. "I don't think he even told me for a few months," said Paul Quigley. "One day he just happened to say he had quit drinking."

The wilder days behind him, Quigley had a new perspective on his golf game: For the first time in his life, he started to believe in his abilities. On April 14, 1997, four days after he turned 50, Quigley played in the Senior PGA Championship. He finished tied for 40th, shooting 10 over par, but was off and running.

Employing a short backswing and his trademark low trajectory, Quigley turned back the clocks by hitting a

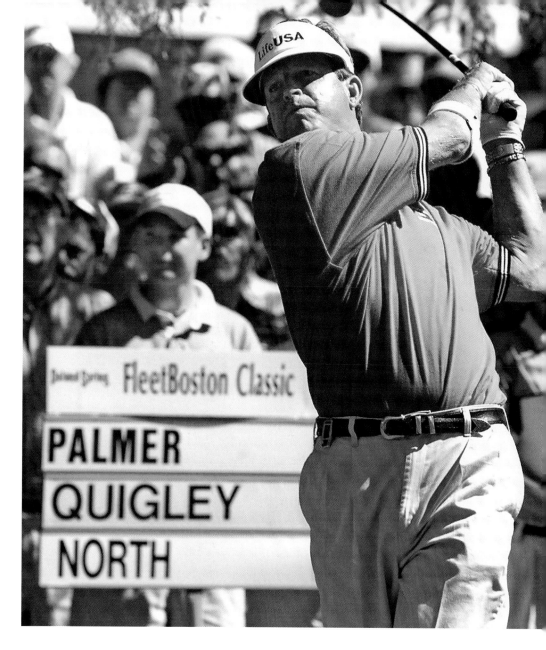

series of Monday qualifiers. Unlike 25 years earlier, this time Dana Quigley had that 15th club in the bag. "Now he believes he's as good as these guys," said the older brother.

In his third event, Quigley was fourth and earned $60,000. A few weeks later, he struck the jackpot, becoming just the sixth Monday qualifier in Senior PGA Tour history to win a tournament.

"I don't feel anything like a star," said the champion. "I feel like the

same guy who was at Crestwood. In some ways, I haven't come to terms with what has happened to me."

Those beer-soaked days long gone, he said he hangs out at the golf course all day and at night usually finds a shopping mall somewhere.

He likes malls? Laugh, if you will, but Quigley couldn't care less. This time around, he's loaded with self-esteem.

"This time around," he said, "I'm in the right league." ♀

The day we discovered golf

DURING A HIGH-PROFILE TOUR of America in 1900, six-time British Open winner Harry Vardon broke the course record in the second day of an exhibition at Vesper Country Club in Tyngsboro, Massachusetts. He reportedly spent the night in a tent along the Merrimack River.

May 20 2000 • By JIM McCABE

The annual Norfolk County Classic is a popular Massachusetts event that dates back several decades, but it isn't the first "classic" event that took place in the hills and valleys of Presidents Golf Club. For that, you have to go back about a century.

Of course, the place was called Wollaston Golf Club in those infant days of American golf. Born in 1895,

Wollaston GC was used by a small group of golfers because the sport had not yet caught the public's fancy. Quite honestly, Americans were mystified by golfing, though that situation started to change thanks to a visit by Harry Vardon in the spring of 1900.

Vardon was referred to as "the champion golfer of the world," having won three of the four previous British Opens with unheard-of scores such as 307 for 72 holes. Local businessmen practically called a work stoppage to get a peek when this phenom made his American debut in Boston.

First, Vardon held an exhibition at the Jordan Marsh department store; the next day — April 18 — he took on some local talent in a pair of matches at Wollaston GC in front of a curious crowd that had traveled to Quincy via train.

They were not disappointed, for Vardon displayed the grip that controlled the swing that produced mammoth drive after mammoth drive.

"Vardon's drive was a corker for 190 yards," read the report in The Boston Globe the next day. Another entry:

"Vardon made as good a drive as he is capable of, getting surely 200 yards." Yet another, describing the par-3 first hole that measured 160 yards: "Vardon, with a midiron, was on the green [while his opponents were 20 and 15 yards short]."

All of this, mind you, without juiced-up balls, a thin-faced driver, and any such thing as a "trampoline effect." (Though he most likely received a "courtesy buggy" somewhere along the line.)

In his exhibitions, Vardon often would take on two players in best ball. In the morning match at Wollaston he defeated Robert Stronnar, a local professional, and A.H. Fenn, 3 and 2, though it was common for players to continue the match out, so it is reported that Vardon prevailed, 5 up.

In the afternoon, the competition was better, though Vardon again won, 1 up, over Clifton Bremer, an amateur at Wollaston, and Alex Campbell, the head pro at The Country Club in Brookline. The match was even (the term "all square" is not mentioned anywhere in the newspaper account) on the 18th hole when Vardon reached the par 4 in regulation and two-putted to beat the bogeys by Bremer and Campbell.

Reported the Globe: "Vardon's exhibitions at Wollaston have thrown a great deal of light on the game, because New England golfers now understand how it is that Vardon stands alone in golf in the old world."

More than a hundred years later, New England golfers understand better than ever how to play this game. The wisest of us have also learned to respect it, and we're grateful to all those who paved the way. ⚲

CHI CHI RODRIGUEZ puts his trademark finishing touch on a birdie putt at the 2000 FleetBoston Classic.

Waverly Oaks
GOLF CLUB

1st TEE
CHAMPIONSHIP
COURSE
→

PING

PLAYING A ROUND

For detailed snapshots of New England's best courses, visit www.explorenewengland.com/golf.

Barrie Bruce
GOLF SCHOOL

A Pair of Sneakers
and a
Good Attitude
→

Ragged
Mountain
Golf Club

RAGGED MT.